"In Judy Esway's *Real Life, Real*
mother who never lived in a conv
ology, who has written a book tha _____ as mon-
umental.

"Out of the grind of everyday joy and loss in a normal ordinary life, Judy Esway develops an extraordinary spirituality.
Great monks, priests, and theologians may by hard work relate
their lofty thoughts to the rest of us mortals. Judy came from the
other direction: she went to lofty sources to help her in daily living. This is the unique, special gift of her book."

Eddie Ensley
Author, *Prayers that Heal Our Emotions*

"Judy Esway's *Real Life, Real Spirituality* is a most inspiring, most
practical, and most exciting book on prayer and spirituality. It's a
beautiful book for the spiritually thirsty. You're going to love each
and every page, and you're going to wish the author could be a
personal friend. Read her book and she will be."

Mitch Finley
Author, *The Gospel Truth: Living For Real in an Unreal World*
and *101 Ways to Nourish Your Soul*

"This is an easy to read introduction to prayer for those who feel
they could never pray or be people of prayer. Judy Esway lets us
know it is not just a matter of 'getting our prayers in'. Prayer has
the potential of being a rich relationship with our loving God, one
that requires time to talk, time to reflect, time to express love, and
time simply to be silent with the one you love. You need to take
the time to *experience* this book and not just read it. Judy Esway is
a good guide."

Fr. Carl J. Arico
Contemplative Outreach

"Here is a summons to prayer with the promise that prayer will change you. No theoretical treatise, it is one woman's experience of the spiritual journey, beginning with conversion and, in her case, a charismatic spiritual awakening, moving through the marvelous changes prayer effects in one's life, and ending with a firm commitment to two periods of contemplative prayer each day. The chapter on spiritual friendship is especially insightful. The methodology is autobiography, the argument, the author's experience, and the style is simple, conversational, and sprightly. This is a book to get people moving in a serious prayer life."

Fr. Ernie Larkin, O.Carm.
Kino Institute
Phoenix, AZ

"From the moment you begin reading and slowly savoring Judy Esway's book (it's too good to rush), you know something about this remarkable woman: she has genuine faith, the kind that cannot be written about without having first been lived. What's more, she has the rare gift of being able to enjoyably communicate what it means to live that lively, insightful faith every day. This is a book worth buying for yourself and then buying another to send to a friend whom you treasure. It's good, and I highly recommend it."

Lou Jacquet
Editor, *Catholic Exponent*
Diocesan newspaper for Diocese of Youngstown, OH

"Many insights from classical and contemporary spiritual masters appear in these pages, complemented by the invitation that readers take time to reflect on their faith and formation journey. The truth is: busy people make God their business. This book tells them how this happens with the help of grace."

Susan Muto, Ph.D.
Executive Director
Epiphany Association

Real Life Real Spirituality

For Busy People Who Want to Pray

Judy Esway

TWENTY-THIRD PUBLICATIONS
Mystic, CT 06355

Twenty-Third Publications
185 Willow Street
P.O. Box 180
Mystic, CT 06355
(860) 536-2611
800-321-0411

ISBN 0-89622-706-5
Library of Congress Catalog Card Number 96-60697
Printed in the U.S.A.

For my soul friends...
my husband, Rick,
Eddie Ensley, John and Bea Valvo,
Vickie Scheer, Sr. Lois Paha, Eileen McCoy,
and my *special* soul friend,
Robert Herrmann

ACKNOWLEDGMENTS

So many wonderful people have influenced me over the years.
Interacting with them has deepened me, made me reflective,
and given me something to write about. I wish to thank them
now.

Our children, René, Valerie, and Rick;
our son-in-law, Terry Batson,
our beautiful granddaughters,
Angela, Caitlin, and Emily;
My mother, Mary Spitale,
and in memory of my father, Coni Spitale;
Our large and colorful Italian families,
the Esways and Spitales,
who keep me grounded and "real";
The courageous and inspiring group
of "self-actualized" women
I meet and pray with each month;
All of my other friends and coworkers
too numerous to mention.
Thank you for touching my life,
just when I needed you.

CONTENTS

INTRODUCTION

This book is about prayer. I write it knowing full well that saints and poets and mystics have written about prayer. I delayed writing it for years because a little nagging voice kept saying, "How could you? How dare you? You're just an ordinary person, a laywoman." But finally it occurred to me that those holy writers must have been ordinary people, too, before they started to pray. I think prayer is what made them saints and poets and mystics.

For years my husband has been urging me to write this book. Even though I've given numerous talks and conducted many workshops on prayer in the past ten years, I still felt unqualified to write about it. My three previous books were reflections, my prayers directed to God; I was comfortable with that. But to write *about* God and how one can have a relationship with God is another matter altogether. Maybe it just wasn't time. But it is now. That's what happens when we pray. We know when the time is right.

My purpose in writing this book is to show how ordinary people, like most of the human population, can live extraordinary lives… if they pray. Saints, poets, and mystics are not born. They once were ordinary people, but something happened to them, something powerful that changed them forever. Well, something happened to me, too, and that is why I dare to write this book.

Too Busy To Pray

Most people think they're too busy to pray. So I've designed this book for busy people, because I understand. I've been a full-time working woman/mother/grandmother (that's a lot of years!) for most of my life and know the juggling routine all too well. But the fruits and enormous benefits of prayer have enticed me to continue the journey, week after week, year after year.

I have discovered, to my great surprise, that when ordinary people pray, they can lead extraordinary lives and *grow* into saints, poets, and mystics. I am talking about *ordinary* people, not special people with halos, but people living busy lives, alternating roles, working hard at relationships and careers, and tending to families. And when enough people are leading extraordinary lives, that's when relationships and families and churches and businesses and entire societies will change. That's when the "peace that surpasses all understanding" will flow gently over our world. That's how the kingdom of God will be ushered in— through one ordinary person after another, after another, after another.

Prayer is not that difficult to do. A little time, a little attention, can yield enormous benefits. When I first started praying, I didn't know what I was doing. I was in spiritual kindergarten. I needed Spirituality 101, and it seemed like every book I picked up was way over my head. I had a hard time finding anything written for "ordinary" people who had just felt the first stirrings of God's Spirit within them.

So wherever you are on the journey, I believe you'll find this book easy to understand. It doesn't mean the material is not profound—it's impossible to speak about prayer in a shallow way— it just means profound truths are expressed in everyday language.

We all have a part to play in making the world a better place. Most of us are not in powerful worldly positions, making decisions that will affect human lives. But we have a more commanding, silent position. We can work from our "home offices"—out of our powerful prayer corners. I may not meet you face to face, saint, poet, mystic, but I promise you this: we will meet in prayer. Day after day, week after week, year after year, we "ordinary" people will meet. And together, we will change the world.

CHAPTER ONE

WHAT IS PRAYER?

"I remember the devotion of your youth, how you loved me as a bride, following me in the desert, in a land unsown" (Jeremiah 2:2). God, how I treasure your words. I, too, remember how I loved you as a bride, your bride. I followed you into the desert of my heart. We traveled into unsown land, carefully, gently making our way together. We had to hack our way through quite a mess before we could even begin to plant. Mostly, I closed my eyes while you pruned and rooted out and prepared the soil. You didn't wait until all of the ground was perfect but only cleared away a little at a time as you scattered your seeds.

I am not a young bride now, God, but my devotion for you hasn't waned. I still trust you as we venture further and further into undeveloped territory. You have proven your faithfulness, God. You never left me alone. You have proven your gentleness. You never pulled a weed from my heart

without soaking it first in the water of your love.
    Where are we going, God? I want to keep going, deeper and deeper and deeper into love.

I had been praying for many years when I wrote this meditation, which appeared in my second book *Womanprayer/ Spiritjourney* (pg. 54). And this image of closing my eyes and following God into the uncharted territory of my heart seemed to be a perfect way to describe prayer. But when I first started praying, I didn't know much about it. I thought it was just a matter of saying the Our Father, Hail Mary, or praying before meals and at bedtime. I honestly didn't think it made much difference if I prayed or not. I just thought I probably should pray since I was born and raised a Catholic. Catholics prayed, so I did too. But secretly I didn't really think anyone was listening to me. And I certainly didn't think anything would change.

But then I started reading about prayer. I read all sorts of books on prayer, struggling through many of them. I read some of the classics like *Interior Castle*, by St. Teresa of Avila; *Dark Night of the Soul*, by St. John of the Cross; and *The Cloud of Unknowing*, author unknown. I read books by modern-day authors like Thomas Keating, Henri Nouwen, Miriam Therese Winter, Eddie Ensley, Maria Harris, John Sanford, Teilhard De Chardin, and Marjorie Holmes, to name a few. And I made the most amazing discovery, something I had never been taught in church or heard anyone say, something so important and valuable that I can't understand why it hasn't been emphasized more. I discovered that there is a close link between spirituality and psychology.

Maybe I'm just slow in "getting it," but when I began to see this link, I could almost believe there might be some kind of power in prayer. And if simply sitting and focusing on God could fix my emotions, and maybe even help my relationships, I knew I'd better get serious about this thing called prayer. Because God knows (and I guess God really did know) that I needed help in both those areas.

So I started to pray, really pray, and I realized what prayer was all about. It is closing our eyes and letting God roam through our lives on every level, straightening out the messes, unraveling the tangled webs, pulling out the weeds, watering, nourishing. Why? So something can grow! I want to keep on growing. I never want to stop, no matter how old I get. So I have asked God to please continue wandering through my life. I've been on my journey for a long time now, and God has already gone to many places inside of me, places where I knew I was hurting. There, I was fully conscious of the pain and fully aware of the "spontaneous healing" following God's tender touch.

But now I have invited God to go deeper, to places I don't even know are there, and to heal me of hurts I don't even know are hurting. Perhaps that deeper pain, just below my consciousness, is what's sapping my energy, holding me back, keeping me fearful too much of the time. All I have to do is keep my eyes closed. God will do the rest. I've learned to trust God. Nothing has surfaced too fast for me to deal with. God's therapy has been perfectly suited to me, to how much I am able to handle, and when I am able to handle it.

If you've been afraid to invite God into your deep heart, you needn't be. God can be trusted. "You have proven your gentleness. You never pulled a weed from my heart without soaking it first in the water of your love."

God will handle you gently too. If only you will trust. God is very much like a close family friend—someone like the woman in the following story.

Mrs. Alonzo's Visits

When I was growing up, my father was sick a lot with rheumatoid arthritis. I remember he'd be upstairs in bed for long periods of time. This took a toll on the family. My mother was nervous and worried with the demands of caring for my dad and wondering how we would survive. And with five small children making one mess after another, the thought of visitors stopping by only made matters worse. Unless, however, that visitor was Mrs. Alonzo.

She was my dad's godmother, a little old Italian lady with the face and disposition of an angel. Mrs. Alonzo would walk from her home up the street from us, stop at the A&P, and trudge down the alley to our house carrying two bags of groceries, all her arms could hold. She'd come in, set the bags on the kitchen table, and go to work.

Everyone loved it when Mrs. Alonzo came to visit. You could see my mother's face soften and relax. It didn't matter if the house was messy or the kids were acting up. Mrs. Alonzo made no judgments. She never asked, "What can I do to help?" She just set the food on the table, greeted all of us warmly, then got busy.

She'd fill the kitchen sink with soapy suds and start washing dishes. Then she'd throw me a towel and say, "Come on, Judita. You dry, we talk. You keep-a me company." Those were peaceful moments for me, and I'm sure for the whole family. I knew Mrs. Alonzo loved me. She loved us all.

I still remember how I felt in the presence of this little Italian lady. As I grew older I'd see her at church or around town, and she'd always greet me warmly. She'd stop her conversation with her lady friends, look right into my eyes, and call me by name. She'd make me feel like I was the most important person in the world. I felt completely at ease with Mrs. Alonzo, completely accepted.

I knew I could trust her, because she loved me. It's like that with God.

Meditation

Take a few moments now and close your eyes. Don't worry if your "house" is a little messy. God wants to visit you. God wants to bring you food and comfort, and even wants to clean your house... a little at a time. All you have to do is be there, keep God company. A little chit-chat, that's all. Whatever you want to talk about will be fine. And if you're not in the mood for talk, that's all right too.

Let God putter around a little. Or you can just sit together for a while. You can feel completely at ease with God. It's just like having Mrs. Alonzo stop by, just that ordinary.

You can go off and do chores for a while if you like, or take a nap, or play with the dog. It feels so good knowing that God is in your house. You sneak a glance every so often, just to make sure God is still there.

God beckons to you and says, "Enough work for today." You walk over and sit next to God, snuggling close. Stay there for a while and relax. Feel God's presence in your body. Breathe love in. Breathe anxiety and fear out. In and out, slowly, gently. Everything will be all right now. God is in your house, taking care of things. Taking care of you.

Rest in God's love, for as long as you wish.

CHAPTER TWO

WHY PRAY?

Why do people pray? What motivates us? After all, it does take a certain commitment, so why should we go to all the trouble? It may seem like a silly question, but it's one that must be asked. "Because Jesus tells us to pray in the Bible," you may answer. True, but why? Why is it so important?

This "why" question has gotten me into a lot of trouble over the years. If I'm asked to do something at work, it has to make sense. I want to know why before I can give it my best effort. Oh, I'll do it, but if I know the purpose, then I'm able to do it with more enthusiasm.

So why do we pray? We know why we eat. We wouldn't live long if we didn't. We know why we exercise. It gives us energy and helps us maintain our weight. We know why we study. We'll have better career opportunities, which in turn could yield a higher quality of life.

These are incentives, strong motivators to put the time and effort into preparing food, taking up exercise, and continuing our education.

With prayer, however, the incentives are less obvious. It's only "after" we've taken up the serious work of prayer (sorry, there *is* an element of work) that occasionally we glimpse that something great may be happening in us. We'll talk more about this in later chapters. For now, let's look at what draws people to prayer when they have no understanding of its power.

Prayer is ultimately a friendship—a friendship with the one who has loved us long before we knew we were loved. We know that even on a human level, wonderful things happen when we're in love. We grow, we become physically and emotionally healthier. We become selfless, even noble at times. And when we're in love, we love everyone else in our lives more deeply too.

Now if this can happen when two human beings fall in love, imagine, just imagine, the possibilities of having a love relationship with God!

Why pray? I'll tell you why I pray. I've fallen in love with God. And yes, there are enormous benefits to prayer, but I didn't know that in the beginning. Even if there were no benefits, I would still pray. Because I want to be with the one I love. I can't not pray. Even if I tried, I don't think I could stop.

My "why" question was answered long ago. And when you know why, then you will want to put your heart and soul into prayer.

Something Changes Us

When I consider my relationship with God before my conversion, my first thought is that God and I were strangers. There was no relationship, no connection. But, of course, that could not possibly be true. God knew everything about me—the color of my hair, the way I moved, the sound of my voice. God knew the little girl, Judy, with the dark, soulful eyes. God knew the adolescent, confused by the strange stirrings of puberty. God knew the young married woman, and the new mother, struggling to find her voice, her femininity, her mission.

I was no stranger to God. God had loved me every moment of my life, and even before. But who was God? I had no idea. I had never met the one who knew me. God was the stranger, not I. Have you ever known someone before they knew you? My husband understands this. He's fond of saying, "I chased Judy until she caught me."

Rick didn't know that someone had been watching him. Oh, he might have had an inkling, a feeling from time to time, but nothing more. We were in high school together, and I fell madly in love with him. But he didn't even know I existed! I just watched him for months. My girlfriends and I would follow him around at school dances and football games, observing how "cool" he was and how well he dressed. And when he'd look our way, we'd quickly turn around and act like we were giggling about something or someone else.

This became serious business to me. I was hopelessly in love and had no idea how to get his attention. Finally, one of his friends found out about it and decided to introduce us. When the time came for me to meet him, I was so nervous I thought I was going to faint. After all the months of watching him from afar, I was now going to see him up close, and he was going to speak my name. After looking at him for so long, he was finally going to look back at me. And when he did, it was even more wonderful than I imagined it would be. I walked on clouds for weeks and months. I had to be the happiest teenager on the planet!

That, to me, is what conversion is all about. It's looking into the eyes of the one who has been looking at us all along, the one who has been yearning for us, dreaming about us, waiting day and night for just one glance from us. And when we finally do look back at God—incredible as it seems—we make God happy!

A Profound Experience

In November of 1977, when I was 38 years old, I had a profound spiritual experience that changed my life forever. It took a lot of years and many little nudges for God to get my attention. God has to play the game just right. A little too fast, a little too intense, and we may be frightened away. So the game is slow and careful, almost like hide-and-seek. Something happens that can't be explained, and we think it might be God. But we're not sure. So we start looking—everywhere. We're more alert now, always listening. Is someone really there?

God sensitizes us for a while, shows us we have nothing to fear. The hide-and-seek game becomes more like a dance, round and round, back and forth. Just when we turn to face our partner, God seems to vanish. But we know someone was there. We know it, we know it, we know it, yet have no idea how we know it.

Then one day, when we're ready, we turn without looking and bump right into God! And this time God does not disappear. Why does God stay? Why now? Why this time? Because God knows we are no longer afraid and won't run away.

My own conversion experience was powerful and life-changing. But please remember my experience of God is unique to me, just as yours is to you. Many people never have a pivotal moment in which they can say they were converted, or awakened, or reborn. Nevertheless, they are very close to God. Some who are Catholic are daily communicants and say they've never had a strong conversion experience. They also say they've always had a strong faith. Does this tell you something? If you're safe in God's home, and you've been filled with faith and trust since you were a child, why would you need a conversion experience? These fortunate people, however, are in the minority.

In his book, *Healing and Wholeness*, John Sanford writes, "Most people do not know God" (72). I really believe that's true. I did not know God until this experience. Oh, of course, I knew *about* God. I'd heard about God my entire life. I'd read about Jesus in the Scriptures. But knowing *about* someone and *knowing* someone are two distinctly different things.

Before my conversion, I went through a long, dark period. I searched for many years, questioning, looking for the meaning of life. John Sanford quotes St. Gregory of Nyssa, "'The soul who is troubled is near unto God'" (8). Sanford concludes, "It sounds as though it is not peace of mind that brings us to wholeness, but struggle and conflict, and spiritual enlightenment occurs only when a person has been through dark and disturbing trials of the soul" (8).

Searching for God

If you've known God for as far back as you can remember, you should rejoice and be grateful. Because it's not that way for everyone. I lost my precious faith and didn't realize the danger I was in until many years after I regained it. I shudder even now when I think of it. I was born and raised Catholic and always went to church. Even the years after I stopped believing, I continued to be a Sunday Catholic. I never missed Mass. Just in case I was wrong, and there really was a God, well, I didn't want to go to hell!

I have fond memories of Catholic grade school, and as a child I had a beautiful, simple faith. But it faded as I got older. There is one especially vivid memory I have of a time when I was still young. I must have been in third or fourth grade. I was sitting in church during Mass, and something struck me as being strange. I looked around at all the people. They had the most serious, dead-pan looks on their faces, yet the words they were speaking were so full of power. In drab, monotone voices they were saying, "And he will come again."

I looked around thinking, who's going to come again? Are they talking about Jesus?

"And we will see him face to face." I started to get a bit excited. We're going to see Jesus face to face?

"And the dead will rise." The dead will rise? You mean we won't have to stay dead? This was good news. This was fantastic news. Why weren't these people smiling? Why weren't they happy?

Finally I heard them say, "And we will live forever." Well, this was really the clincher. We're going to live forever? Why weren't they dancing in the aisles? Why weren't they clapping and shouting if they were going to live forever? On that sad day it dawned on me: these people must not believe what they are saying. And so I stopped believing it too.

After grade school, I went to a public high school where I met my husband. I was fifteen and he was seventeen, and we started going steady. Shortly after high school, Rick and I got married. The years went on and we were living a rather nice life. We had three healthy children, lived in a nice house, and Rick and I had a pretty good relationship, nothing like it is now, of course. We didn't have the emotional or spiritual depth to our marriage that we have today. But we were young, and things were pretty much okay.

Then when I moved into my mid-thirties, a strange thing started to happen. A certain sadness swept over me. It took me by surprise, because I didn't have any serious problems. By the world's standards, I had no reason to be so sad. But little by little, the normal things that people did gave me no satisfaction. We went to dinner with our friends, played cards, went to movies, did things with our children. But everything left me empty. I remember that when I would hear beautiful music I would cry because I felt so sad. Once when I saw a magnificent sunset it left me feeling devastated. I know now it was because I didn't know the creator of this beauty. And somehow I felt left out, disconnected, floundering all alone.

The sadness grew deeper and turned to depression. If you've ever been seriously depressed, you know how debilitating it can be. And you can't just will it away. You can't even pray it away, because when you're depressed you can't pray. And I had almost stopped praying altogether by that time anyway. I became withdrawn and isolated. I wasn't working at the time, which made it worse. If I had been forced to go out of the house every day to a job, maybe it would have been better. But I just stayed in the house and didn't go out unless I absolutely had to. I didn't seek help. I didn't even tell anyone how awful I felt. I just thought I was going through a bad time and it would pass. And in those days, people didn't go for counseling as easily as we would today. Even Rick didn't know how seriously depressed I was. I hid it from him, just as I did from everyone else. No one knew that inside I was dying a slow death.

One of my darkest moments came late at night, after cleaning our old green couch. Spring cleaning was big in those days, and I did it with a vengeance. From morning to night, for weeks, I cleaned every drawer and closet, every room, every little nook and cranny. Rick and the kids had been in bed for hours, and I was still scrubbing the couch. I finally finished, exhausted, and walked into the kitchen in tears. Why was I doing this? Why was I doing anything? Nothing made any sense.

I felt engulfed in a thick, black cloud when a frightening vision popped into my mind. I saw a long line of little people, almost like stick people. They were going about their business, living their daily lives, and then one by one, I saw them fall to the ground and die. I was in that line. And I, too, would someday drop and die. And who would ever care that I had just scrubbed that stupid green couch? Who would care about anything I'd ever done? I felt like my life had no meaning.

What followed was the first move in the game—the hide-and-seek game I told you about. God saved me that night. In that moment, when I was as close to some sort of emotional death as I had ever been, God saved me. I know this may sound strange, but just when I thought my life had no meaning, "something" came through my kitchen window and went straight to the center of my heart. I felt it. It was a physical sensation of gentle electricity that seemed to come in a ray, through the window, right into my heart.

My Life Had Meaning

I was instantly healed. I knew at that precise moment that I *was* important, that my life did have meaning, and that everything would be well, that I would be well. I stood there for what seemed like a long time, transfixed. Then I switched off the kitchen light, went quietly up to bed, and slept like a baby. The next morning I was filled with peace and joy and laughter. I felt emotionally sound for the first time in years.

Did I know God then? Not yet. I was in the early stage, where the game is slow and careful. I knew that something wonderful had happened to me, and I thought it had to be God. So I started looking for God—everywhere. I even tried to pray again.

One night I found myself voicing an unusual prayer. It was a simple prayer, and it wasn't the kind of prayer I would normally pray. At that time I might say an Our Father or Hail Mary, but that's all. This prayer came from beyond me.

I said, "God, please give me spiritual growth." That's all I said. I remember thinking, I don't even know if there is a God. I thought the "electricity" in the kitchen had to be God, but if it had been God, where did God go? I said it again, "God, please give me spiritual growth." The words just spilled out of my mouth. I looked up at the ceiling and all around the room and said, "If anybody's out there, please give me spiritual growth."

I don't know how long I prayed that prayer. It could have been a year, maybe two. Every night I said it and it never expanded. "God, please give me spiritual growth." I never told anyone. I just repeated that prayer every day. It was such a strange thing to be saying, because I didn't know if there was such a thing as spiritual growth. I knew there was emotional growth, and intellectual, and physical. But spiritual? What was spiritual?

After a long time, something started to happen. Slowly. I can't explain it adequately. I've tried many times. I can only liken it to a rumbling inside of me, a stirring, a waking up. The world around me seemed to have put on a brighter garment; I saw new and beautiful colors everywhere I looked. For a while, I thought the world was waking up, too, but I was the one who had been sleeping.

This wondrous thing was happening to me, and I didn't understand it. I had no vocabulary to describe it. I had never heard anyone talk about a spiritual conversion or spiritual awakening. Not in those days. And even if I could have found words for it, I didn't know who to talk to about it, except my husband. I tried to tell him, "Something is happening to me, I can't explain it. I feel like I've been dead for a long time, but now I'm coming back to life!" Rick didn't understand it either, but he loved me and believed me. And he could see how much happier I was. He could see there was a joy bubbling up inside of me.

Ironically, I had no Christian friends to talk to about this. I know that's hard to believe, but it's true. I had a lot of Catholic friends, and that's not to put them down, believe me. It's just to say they were like me. They went to church on Sunday, didn't eat meat on Friday, sent their kids to Catholic school, but none of us had a personal relationship with God. If any did, they never told me about it. We never once talked about God. We talked about our children and our card club and the latest movies. We exchanged recipes and talked about spring cleaning and who was going on vacation. But we never talked about God. I never talked to anyone about God! About that time I attended a weekend retreat, hoping to find people I could talk to. I needed to tell someone about this "life" flowing into me.

Seeing with New Eyes

I needed to talk about the day I was sitting in our backyard, looking at our huge tree. The tree startled me, as if it had come out of nowhere. Had it sprung up overnight?

The tree, of course, had always been there, but I had never seen it before. Oh, I had seen it before, but I had never *really seen* it before. It was the most beautiful tree in the world. It looked alive. It seemed to pulsate, as if it were filled with vibrations. I just sat there, stunned, in awe of this magnificent tree. God was there, right in my backyard, right in my tree! Other things were happening. The children looked more beautiful and precious; my husband was so kind. The grass and the flowers had the sweetest fragrance, and the colors were vivid and bright.

Another day, in a hallway of a hospital where I had taken a part-time job, I saw a pot full of fresh flowers sitting on a small table. The flowers were a color I had never seen before! I looked long and hard at them, in wonder, puzzled. I returned to them, time and again throughout my shift, and could not tell what color they were. They were breathtaking, lovely beyond words—a color I have not seen since. I can't even say whether it was blue, purple, or green. It was not like anything I had ever seen! I wonder to this day if God put those flowers there just for me, to let me know there is more, so much more to life.

When I attended the retreat, I found people I could tell my stories to. They just smiled, knowingly, when I babbled on about the tree, and the vibrations in my kitchen, and the color I couldn't name. After two days of inspiring talks by laymen and women as well as clergy, a group of people prayed with me.

I can't tell you what happened, but something did. And I always hesitate to talk about it, because people experience God in many different ways. In the blink of an eye, you may suddenly know you've come in contact with the Divine. It could be so quiet, so natural. All you did was blink your eyes, like you've done billions of times, but this time, your eyes opened to a brand new world. Everything was different. You were different.

For others, it's a slow awakening, perhaps over a lifetime. God gives us what we need. I was so lost for so long that God must have felt I needed a strong experience. I needed to know that God was real and that I was loved. The only way to explain what happened while prayers were being offered all around me that afternoon was that I finally saw God, not with my eyes, but with some other way of seeing. I looked back at God, and this time God did not vanish. I even think I made God happy!

I went home that evening, ecstatic. I could sense God's presence inside me, and I knew that my life would never be the same.

From Knowing *about* God to Knowing God

One thing I learned from my spiritual awakening is that there are three commonly held, totally false beliefs.

Belief number one: "I can't be a religious person. I'm not good enough. I have to straighten up first." That's what I thought, even after I had the powerful encounter with God. Maybe I should try to slow this thing down, I worried. I need time—to read the Bible, to become a better wife and mother, to forgive the people who had hurt me, and to ask forgiveness from those I'd hurt, and on and on and on.

I was looking at a daunting task! And I had no idea where to begin. Then I read something wonderful. I didn't have to clean myself up—that was God's job. And furthermore, God loved me—just the way I was, exactly the way I was—and didn't really want to wait any longer. Now was the time. God had called me! This news was almost too good to be true. What a relief. So I simply started, every day, sitting in my prayer chair, before I knew anything about prayer. I would say, "Here I am, God, here I am." I'd make no apologies for my condition; it didn't seem necessary. God would take care of all those mundane details in time.

Belief number two: "I'm afraid to get too religious. God might change my personality. I might have to move to China and become a missionary. And I know I'd never have fun again!" My husband knew that God was calling him. And although the attraction was growing stronger, Rick resisted and fought and avoided it. I couldn't understand it, until he finally opened up about his fears. "I'm really afraid, Jude," he said.

"Of what?"

"I just know I'll have to go knocking on doors carrying a big Bible, and I'll have to wear a huge cross around my neck. And I don't want to do that. Or what if we have to move somewhere and become missionaries? That's just not me."

I chuckle now when I remember our conversation, but Rick was dead serious. I convinced him (don't ask me how) that God doesn't make us do anything that's out of character for us. Rick's an introvert by nature. And now, many years into his spiritual journey (yes, he finally gave in), he's still an introvert. His "missionary" work has been quiet—in ordinary places, like at work and among our families. He doesn't talk as much about God as I (the extrovert); he's just developed into a gentle, peaceful presence, a Christ bearer.

So if you're afraid to give your life to God, you really needn't be. God gave you your personality. And God will respect it and keep it intact. There won't be any drastic changes that will frighten you or make you terribly uncomfortable. You'll just become more of who you already are. Your deep, true self—the *you* you know you can be—will emerge ever so slowly. However, if you want to go to China, or go knocking on doors carrying a big Bible, it certainly can be arranged. That may spark your interest and suit you perfectly. God will let you do whatever you want to do.

Belief number three: "I'm afraid to give my life to God. I just know trouble will come my way." I can't argue this one. Trouble will come your way. But guess what? Trouble will come your way anyhow. And I'd rather have God in my life when trouble comes than try to go through it alone. Trials and difficulties can then take on some meaning. We're being perfected. We're learning through the tough times. We're growing. It does appear, however, that some people do experience a lot of difficulties shortly after finding God. I've thought a lot about this, and I had a wonderful insight that really made sense to me.

We Reap What We Sow

It's got to do with sowing seeds. We know we reap what we sow. It's a natural and spiritual law. And if there were years when we didn't have a relationship with God, perhaps we had sown a lot of bad seed. Maybe we made poor decisions, burned bridges, severed important relationships, didn't take care of our physical, emotional, and financial lives. I saw this in the form of an image. I was walking down a certain path, and all the consequences of my "sowing" were following me, right at my back. Then, when I was "awakened," suddenly I stopped and turned to walk a new path. On this path I would sow new and better seeds, because God would show me how to live a good life. But what about all I had already sown? Would those consequences go away overnight? Oh, how I wish.

No. They came right at me and hit me square in the back when I stopped. And I had to deal with them and make them right. And I was so glad I had God to show me how to do it. But before the troubles came, right after my conversion, I was so high I floated for months. I honestly thought following God would be one long series of warm fuzzies. I didn't know God was going to *ask* something of me! When I came back down to earth, I sensed God saying, "Now, Judy, let's look at your life. How about this relationship over here."

"Well... uh ...I guess it does need a little work, God," I muttered.

Later, another nudge. "Now, let's go back to this area of your life."

"Oh, no, wait, God. That's too painful."

"I'll go back with you, daughter. Don't be afraid."

Still later, "Let's work on forgiving and getting rid of that grudge you've been holding for so long against—you know."

So this is the "work" of prayer. Mostly it comes in straightening out our relationships, in forgiving, asking forgiveness, and the hardest one of all—letting go. But after a long time, we begin to feel happy and light again. The more we cooperate in this process, the faster it will happen. God takes no joy in our troubles and difficulties. Most of them (not all) are because of those seeds we've sown while we were still sleeping. God wants us to live in peace and harmony. I really believe we're the ones who slow things down by resisting change, by holding onto our old ways, even when we know they've brought us a lot of trouble.

And yet we need to be patient with ourselves. Our new path is unfamiliar, and it will take a little time to learn how to behave differently. And it will take time to really believe we can trust God. But when we know it, deep down in our bones, look out, world! Anything is possible. Marvelous, exciting things will happen... and to our great surprise, they will happen through us!

Meditation

Take a few moments now and reflect on a spiritual experience you have had. It may have been subtle. Perhaps you could relate to my "hide and seek" story. Maybe there have been times in your life when you knew God was there, but had no idea how you knew it. And maybe, just maybe, you've been the one hiding because you weren't ready. Or maybe you thought that God would ask too much of you. Or maybe you weren't convinced that you could trust God.

Think about one of those close encounters (we've all had them). Close your eyes and enter once again into that experience, that memory, that feeling of being cherished. It may have lasted only a moment, because you (or God) went right back into hiding. But it carried enormous healing power and left you with a feeling of deep peace and a "knowing."

Let that feeling once again surround and embrace you. Let the dance become a slow dance now, and speak to your partner, without words, about all that is in your heart.

CHAPTER THREE

PRAYER CHANGES OUR LIVES

After my dramatic encounter with God at the retreat, my feet didn't touch the ground for months. Being spiritually high, walking on clouds, is wonderful. But if your life doesn't change, and you're not growing in love, what good is it? When you float back down to earth, you'd better have something to show for it. Did you really meet God? Or was it just some sort of hallucination?

The only way you can know for sure is if your life changes. It's the only measure you can trust. My life changed dramatically. To prove it I'll have to tell you the situation I came home to after the retreat.

My mother-in-law was living with us at the time. She was born in Italy and had come to this country when she was twenty-seven years old, after she married my father-in-law. His first wife died in childbirth with their seventh child. He had later gone back to his hometown in Italy and married Elena. When they arrived in America, Elena was in for a shock. Nothing could have prepared her for what she found: a small run-down house and a group of sad little children returning from temporary stays in orphanages and homes of friends.

There were huge problems. Communication (Elena spoke only Italian), culture shock, homesickness, and a ready-made family with urgent, pressing needs. But somehow she survived, raised the children, and gave birth to seven more!

I married the fourteenth, her baby.

Mom and I got along fairly well over the years, but it was difficult. She was a dynamic woman who made a deep impression on everyone who met her. She was colorful, spontaneous, and totally unpredictable. But she drove us all crazy—she was impossible! My father-in-law had passed away the year before I made the retreat, and Mom didn't want to live alone. She needed to find a place to stay and was trying everyone out. This was our turn. I think it was our second or third turn. (She thought she should give us another chance.)

Mom would stay for a while, then she'd get mad at something and go home. Soon she'd be back, get mad again, and demand we drive her home, in stony silence all the way. She didn't sell her house, just in case. So this was one of the times she was back with us again.

I wrote about my feelings toward her—before and after my retreat—years ago in an article for *New Covenant* magazine. I share excerpts from that article with you here to show you how dramatically my life changed.

I walked into the house that night—or should I say floated in—a new person. I felt flushed, excited, deeply happy. I had just come home from a renewal weekend at our church where I had discovered a whole new relationship with the Lord. Jesus had come alive to me that night, and I knew I would never be the same.

My husband and the children were watching television

with my mother-in-law. They seemed to be different, too. Very different. They looked so beautiful, so precious.

My mother-in-law had just finished making noodles, and she had that crazy bandanna on her head that she always wore when she made noodles. It was tilted and falling down over her forehead. It made her look so charming. Funny, but I had never thought of my mother-in-law as charming before. It was all I could do to keep myself from running over to her and hugging her and telling her that I loved her. What a ridiculous thought, I told myself. I certainly couldn't do that, not to my mother-in-law.

She lived life with a passion; she did everything with gusto. If she liked you she would give you all she had. And you always knew how much she liked you by how many choice Italian names she called you. I was very high on her list.

Mom took great pride in her cooking, and rightly so, for her spaghetti sauce, ravioli, homemade noodles, veal cutlets, and manicotti were wonderful. In her usual *modest* way she would say, "I'm-a da best-a cook in the whole world. Nobody touch-a me, boy."

She could go into ecstasy over a plump chicken. One day she put one in our kitchen sink to clean it and started going crazy over the perfect chicken she had found. She kept going back and forth saying, "God-a bless, God-a bless, you beauuuutiful chicken. Ma guarda ['just look']. Quanta bella, beauuuutiful chicken."

She'd walk away for a minute to do something else, but the chicken kept calling her back, and she'd start the whole thing over again.

After about twenty minutes of this, I said, "Okay, Mom. It's only a chicken." Well, for some reason, she didn't like my insulting her chicken, so she yelled as loud as she could. "Sai zitta ['shut up'], you stupidona."

She liked me.

In Italy, when families lived together, the oldest person was the boss. So Mom naturally felt that she was supposed to be the boss in this new arrangement. Before Rick and I knew what was happening, it was too late. It was a constant battle to keep control of the children and our own lives. She was such a strong person that even both Rick and I together couldn't win. She could outtalk us, outwit us, outcharm us, and definitely outyell us. Most of the time we would just let her win. It was easier that way.

We couldn't even go out together for an evening without a confrontation. On our way out the door she would yell at us, "You come-a home early, understand?" We'd say, "Mom, we're almost forty years old. You can't tell us what to do." And she'd yell loud enough for the whole neighborhood to hear, "I'm-a no give a [blankety blank] how old-a you are. You come-a home early." We'd go out the door all huffy and humiliated. "How did we get into this?" we asked ourselves.

We had been going on like this for months before I made the renewal retreat at our parish. And now, as I stood looking at her with her crazy scarf falling down over her face, seeing her as God sees her, something happened to me. I thought to myself, "I love her." It startled me. "I really love my mother-in-law, who has taken over my entire world."

Beginning that day, my relationship with Mom became very deep. We had something special. We still had our moments of anger, but they didn't last very long. We became close friends. We had so much fun together, kidding around, and trying to outwit one another. When she would go out to play cards with her friends, I would holler, "You be home early, understand?"

She'd laugh and say, "I'm-a old. Nobody tell me what to do, boy."

I'd yell louder, "I said you be home early, Mom. I don't care how old you are!"

She'd go out the door laughing, "Judita, you craze, that's-a be shoo."

I didn't realize it, but Rick was quietly observing us for months. Most of the time he was upset and angry at something his mom had done. But I had so much peace; I was able to laugh it off. One day he said to me, "Judy, I want what you have. Anyone that can get along with my mother has got to have something special, and I want it, too."

So who do you think changed? Not my mother-in-law! Hardly! I did. Because I had welcomed the Holy Spirit into my life, I suddenly had the power to change, to bend, to be flexible and accepting. This is the perfect test, the only test, to see if our spiritual experience was real. Did we truly meet God? There's only one way to be sure. And that's if our lives change and we're growing in love.

I tell you this story, not only because I think everyone deserves to meet my mother-in-law, but to demonstrate in a concrete way that prayer can profoundly change us. If our life doesn't change, we are not really praying. Our prayer life isn't real. We may be tricking ourselves, getting caught up in the "idea" of God rather than coming before the "living" God and making a serious commitment.

But worst of all (or maybe best of all), God is still waiting for us. It's never, ever too late. So what if it didn't seem to work the first time. Seek God again. Be honest. "Here I am, God, just as I am." God will not disappoint. And even though we think our time has passed, it can never pass. The time is now. Always now. We have to go after God as if we are searching for buried treasure.

Prayer Makes Us Treasure Hunters

"The kingdom of heaven is like a treasure buried in a field, which a person finds and hides again, and out of joy goes and sells everything to buy that field" (Mt 13:44). That was me. I searched for years in field after field, not even knowing what I was looking for. Did you ever have the nagging feeling that there was more, and that you were missing it?

One day, as I was sifting through the rubble of my life, my eyes caught a glimpse of something shiny. I was straining to see it when the dirt shifted and covered it. Perhaps I had only imagined it. But later, I saw it again. Something was gleaming! If only I could push the dirt away, slowly, carefully, I might be able to reach it. There it was! A treasure in my hands. I couldn't believe my good fortune. I went away rejoicing. Suddenly all I had once thought important seemed nothing compared to this. The treasure was God, hiding right here—in me. What a truly unbelievable find!

Prayer is like going on a treasure hunt. Sounds exciting, doesn't it? But I must warn you that digging for buried treasure can get a little messy. We have to be willing to get our hands dirty. And digging for buried treasure can be awfully tedious, even boring at times. It requires patience and perseverance. And sometimes we may have to lower ourselves down into a dark, messy hole. But if we go slowly, carefully, we'll catch glimpses of it—the treasure within us. It will gleam and catch our eye. It may even blind us momentarily with its beauty.

And when we can see again, we know that nothing will ever stop us. We couldn't turn back if we tried, not after we've tasted heaven.

Prayer Helps Us to Mature

I'm sure you've met some young people who are wiser and far more mature than some older people. Unfortunately, growing old does not seem to guarantee emotional maturity. In the same way, prayer does not guarantee spiritual maturity. We could pray all day and all night and never grow if we're not open to change. I know people who pray often, and yet they're so hard on their children. They refuse to let them go.

When we're serious about God, we have to say yes to the changes that will take place in our lives. And when we persist in prayer, even if it's only ten or fifteen minutes a day, we will mature and be healed if we're open to this transformation. I don't know how it happens, but little by little, we become healthy, grounded, and wise.

True prayer, honest prayer, doesn't make us pious, or sweet and syrupy. It does not fill us with clichés and Bible quotes that we can throw at others to prove our point. And being wise does not mean we know more. It means just the opposite. It means we can't give pat answers anymore. Real prayer makes us real people. It makes us more human. We enter more deeply into the mystery of life. We grapple more with it. We have more questions.

I'm sorry if you expected to have more answers. I did too. But what I have are pieces of a fascinating, intricate puzzle. I also expected to have more control over my world, not less. But it's not as stressful this way. It feels wonderful not to have to be in control, not to have to have all the answers—as if I ever did!

What I *did* get more of after all these years was faith and trust and a life full of surprises. When I'm not afraid, God can be spontaneous with me, playful. But only as long as I remain open to the changes going on in me. A "new me" is being formed, and I have to get to know me. How will this new me think and act? There are new tapes playing in me now. The former tapes are old, outdated, and oh, so boring. Go ahead now. Give up control and let God work in you. Live dangerously for a change. Believe me when I tell you it's the safest way to go.

Prayer Heals Our Wounded Emotions

A friend of mine, Eddie Ensley (about whom I'll say more later), wrote a wonderful book titled *Prayer That Heals Our Emotions.* He describes healing prayer like this:

It involves finding that we have so many inner resources that we've buried and forgotten about. So, a part of inner healing is reconnecting with these parts of ourselves. It's like coming to a family reunion and sitting down at a table and seeing aunts and uncles and cousins that you haven't seen in a long time. Well, we kind of sit down at a table in healing prayer and get in touch with parts of ourselves that we have forgotten about, that we did not acknowledge were there.

Thomas Keating, in his book *Open Mind, Open Heart*, calls it divine psychotherapy (93). I needed divine therapy. Since I've been praying, the most significant changes in my life have been in the realm of my emotions. I experienced a lot of inner healing—it happened automatically as I prayed. I didn't have to choreograph it. I didn't have to list all my wounded parts. I simply closed my eyes every day and let God go to places inside me that I didn't even know were there, to heal me of hurts I didn't even know were hurting. We don't have to understand it all. We can't understand it all, because so much of it lies in our unconscious where we've buried it, perhaps because the pain was too great.

There may be days when we feel irritable and don't know what's bothering us. We may want to snap at everyone who dares to cross our path. I remember one morning at work, someone said a little too brightly, "Good morning. How's everyone this morning?" I wanted to scream at him and tell him to take his sunshine elsewhere. At the end of the day, I realized that God was "disturbing" me, deep down. I felt all day as if I were undergoing some sort of operation and was under a light anesthesia, not knowing exactly what the surgeon was doing but aware that something was going on.

So when you pray, sometimes you'll feel sad or uncomfortable and not know why. Just let it be. God is healing you. And if it's best for you to know what's happening, you'll know. But trust God to know what's best. When the surgery is over, you may simply feel better—lighter, with a sense of joy. You won't always know why, and you don't really need to know.

There may also be long periods when you don't feel "disturbed" at all. You'll think God must not be able to find anything else wrong with you! Then one day you run into that person—you know who, the one you always avoid, the one you've been holding a grudge against for so long. You've tried. You've honestly tried to forgive and see some good in him or her. Could you help it if goodness just wasn't there? But this time, for a second or two, he or she seems almost beautiful to you. In a flash, you see something wonderful. You may even share a laugh together. And you wonder why you could never see anything like this before, and why you always cringed at the sight of that person.

But the Healer, the mender of people and relationships, is always working in us. Whether we know it or not, whether we feel it or not, whether we remember it or not, God continues to work in us. "It is God's will that we grow in holiness" (1 Thes 4:3), and so we can expect marvelous healing and transformation to occur over time. However, there may be areas of our lives we will struggle with until the day we die. "Three times I begged the Lord that this [suffering] might leave me" (2 Cor 12:8).

Perhaps God deliberately leaves us with something to keep us humble. How can we be compassionate toward others if we haven't had our own ongoing struggles? I've found great comfort in God's answer to Paul. "My grace is enough for you, for in weakness power reaches perfection" (2 Cor 12:9). This is not to say certain thorny areas won't improve. But we may have a negative pattern of behavior that comes and goes throughout our lives. It may reappear when we're under stress from our jobs, when we reach mid-life, or when we find ourselves widowed and alone. "Oh, no," we'll say. "Not you again. I thought you were gone forever."

And the battle begins one more time. But God promises to get us through it. It will not conquer us as it did in the past. It will simply be a "thorn in our side." Yes, we would love to pull it out altogether, because it's uncomfortable and embarrassing! But we can live with it because of God's grace. And when we accept that we're entirely dependent on God to help us, suddenly it's better. It doesn't hurt so much. But we know it's still there. Perhaps it's something we've inherited, just as we've inherited our blue or brown or green eyes. It's a part of us that may be with us until the day we die. But it won't incapacitate us anymore, because God is with us now.

During these periods when our "thorn" acts up, our task is to resist the temptation to think all is lost, that we've made no progress after all this time. While it may seem that way, it is not true! It's a lie! Don't believe it! The best antidote to this lie is to think about how far you've come. "The favors of the Lord I will recall, the glorious deeds of the Lord..." (Is 63:7). The changes in you may have been so gradual that you don't even realize you're a different person now.

We're all familiar with the story of the ten lepers. I thought I knew everything there was to know about this parable. But have you ever read a familiar Scripture passage and suddenly seen something you've never seen before? It feels something like a lightning bolt. Where on earth did that come from? That's how I felt when I read this:

> When he saw them, he responded, "Go and show your-selves to the priests." On their way there they were cured. One of them, *realizing* that he had been cured, came back praising God in a loud voice... Jesus took the occasion to say, "Were not all ten made whole? Where are the other nine?" (Lk 17:14–15,17).

This time the word *realizing* nearly jumped off the page at me. "One of them, *realizing* that he had been cured..." I had never noticed that before. It occurred to me that maybe the others just hadn't realized they were cured. And maybe the reason they did-n't was because they were so used to being the way they were. Maybe they couldn't fathom being any different, that they could be healed. Oh, yes, they had found Jesus and asked to be healed, but don't we do that all the time? How often do we really believe it will happen? It's difficult to imagine that any real change could ever happen in us. It could happen in other people, but not us. So when God does cure us, we may not even *realize* it.

Often our own healing, our transformation, comes gradually, ever so slowly, and we only realize we're different when we look back over the years and recall the "favors of the Lord, the glori-ous deeds of the Lord. Because of his love and pity, he redeemed them himself, lifting them and carrying them all the days of old" (Is 63:9). So in the beginning of our journey God lifts us and car-ries us, because we don't know how to change. But we know we need to, and we want to. Nevertheless, we can't. We're incapable of it on our own. We must trust that God will not abandon us along the way, especially when the "thorn" in our side begins to act up, "...the Lord keeps faith; he it is who will strengthen you..." (2 Thes 3:3).

So if you slip back into your old behavior for a time, don't think all is lost. Think about how far you've come. Remember all the marvelous changes that have taken place in your life because you remained faithful to prayer. You're a different person now! Remember and be grateful.

Prayer Helps Us Give Up Control

Real prayer helps us to let go of others. It breaks the cycle of control and manipulation—finally. For some people, this is very difficult. Being Italian, I know a lot about manipulation and guilt trips. As with many ethnic groups, it's in our genes! We grew up with it. We have been in training for it our whole lives. We had to learn it so we could pass it down, right along with the recipe for spaghetti sauce. It's an art! And I was just getting good at it when I started to pray. Now this wonderful "talent" that took me years to perfect was going to waste.

Because God respects us so much, we learn to respect others, to give them their space. We can finally stop barging in. God never barges in, but rather comes gently knocking at the door, saying, "I'm here. I will always be here, waiting for you, loving you. When you're ready, all you need to do is open the door."

When we pray, we learn to honor our adult children and respect their individuality and the choices they make. We learn to trust their inner guide as easily as we now trust ours. And when we can do that, a wonderful thing happens. Our children become our friends. Prayer has helped me to let go of my children. I don't want them to dread coming home for the holidays because suddenly they feel like they're twelve years old again. I want them to *want* to come home and be treated like the adults they are. I want them to be relaxed when they're with us and have fun. Prayer has brought me to this point.

Unfortunately, I can still regress from time to time, like when our daughter quit college and announced she was moving to San Francisco to become a singer. Suddenly I remembered my "art." My old martyr voice came back to me so quickly. How well I remember that day. I wrote the following reflection and have read it to many groups. The response is always the same—people nodding, smiling, and always a few tears. Invariably women will come up after my talk and tell me stories of their own painful struggles to let go of their children. Somehow it helps to know that this is a universal experience.

It's been several years now since our daughter, Valerie, abruptly moved out of her college dorm, drove home from Flagstaff and announced, "Mom and Dad, I'm quitting school and moving to San Francisco to become a singer!"

Her father and I thought she was just home on spring break, so it took a minute to sink in. Rick recovered first and choked, "Excuse me?" I was confused. "I beg your pardon, you're going to become a what?"

"A singer," she smiled.

I was still confused. "But I've never heard you sing once, not in your whole life, not even in the shower!"

"I know, but I do, and it's my dream. Don't try to talk me out of it, Mom. I have to follow my heart."

"But they have earthquakes in San Francisco... and we'll be paying on your student loans for years—you were supposed to take them after you graduate—and... you don't have any money, and..." I felt faint.

"Mom, I'll get a job and as soon as I get settled I'll pay the loans. Don't worry." I panicked. "Val, you can't go. The earthquakes."

"Earthquakes are exciting!"

"Not if you die in one!"

"Mom, when it's my time, it's my time."

Rick rallied when he remembered he was an Italian father. "You're not going, young lady, and that's that."

"Dad, you can't stop me. I'm nearly twenty-one."

"Well," he sputtered. "Well then..."

"After all we've done for you," I said in my best martyr voice.

"Mom, not a guilt trip. You're above that."

"Flattery will get you nowhere. We'll talk about it tomorrow."

"Mom, there's nothing to talk about. I'm going."

She did go, and with our blessing as it should be. How often I've quoted the great poet Gibran on children—maybe I shouldn't have in front of *our* children! "You may give them your love but not your thoughts, for they have their own thoughts. You may house their bodies but not their souls, for their souls dwell in the house of tomorrow, which you cannot visit, not even in your dreams."

We had to let Valerie go and we both knew it. And we had to support her emotionally and tell her we admired her courage. Maybe the world would be a better place if everyone followed their hearts. Maybe we'd all be in the right place at the right time doing what God hoped we would. For isn't it God who plants dreams deep in the heart of each person? And so we prayed: "Here's a little love offering, God, our Valerie, a gem for your precious 'house of tomorrow.'"

Letting go of our children may be the most difficult challenge many of us will ever have to face. But we have no right to hold onto them. God has trusted us to love them, raise them, and give them back when it's time. God has a plan for their lives as well as our own, and the health of the world depends on the fulfillment of our children's dreams. We simply must let them follow their hearts, even when we don't understand and it scares us to half to death. God has trusted us. Now it's our turn to let go and trust God.

Valerie has worked long and hard to make her dreams come true; waitressing during the day—writing songs, practicing, and performing in the evening. It's starting to pay off for her. She just recorded her first record and went on a short tour to promote it. She and her band are now getting booked into better clubs and receiving good press coverage. Who knows? We may even get some of that student loan money back someday. (You didn't really think she would pay it back, now did you?)

Prayer Makes Us Peaceful

As my prayer deepened into contemplative prayer, amazing things happened. I moved into a place of peace, joy, and a bubbling enthusiasm about life. But do you know what I had to go through before I came to that place? A jungle. The jungle was my heart, the wild, tangled mess of my life.

I was afraid of the jungle. So all I did was close my eyes and hoped my inner guide, the Holy Spirit, knew the terrain. Later, looking back, I realized how much of the jungle had been cleared and how much healing had taken place. Some of it was deep, and I was barely conscious of God's movement there. We're not usually aware of how much these festering wounds are affecting our behavior and health until after God touches and heals us. As God moves, we begin to sense an inner calm. A peace, not so easily disturbed, takes root.

This peace will make us gentle, but it doesn't mean we'll become doormats. Quite the opposite. People who pray are strong and assertive when the situation calls for it. They know they deserve respect, because they have become aware of their immense value. They discover they are God's treasure! "Whoever touches you touches the apple of my eye" (Zec 2:12).

Can a mother forget her infant, be without tenderness for the child of her womb? Even should she forget, I will never forget you. See, upon the palms of my hands I have written your name (Is 49:15,16).

When I used to pray for peace in the world, I thought it was useless. I felt powerless, and I thought my prayer was powerless, too. The world was in too much of a mess. What could one person do? But I found I could do a lot toward bringing peace to the world by bringing peace to *my* world, beginning with me. As I prayed, the different warring factions inside of me came together. Old hurts were forgiven and healed. I began to trust again, trust myself, because I knew God was real and I was loved deeply.

My new calm and centered self could then spill over into my corner of the world. If I can only make my tiny corner peaceful, and you can make your tiny corner peaceful, the two will merge and flow out. A quiet ripple begins, the same as when a tiny pebble is tossed into a lake. It moves slowly, with great precision, out as far as the eye can see. Nothing can stop it! Do you see how important this work of prayer is? One person can go a long way in bringing peace to the world. There's great wisdom in the beautiful song, "Let there be peace on earth, and let it begin with me."

After (and while) our own warring factions are making peace, we look toward mending our relationships. In our family we stopped avoiding our problems and started to confront them. It meant pain. Many people go to great extremes to avoid pain. They spend their whole lives running from confrontation, burying feelings of anger, hurt, and frustration. But when we protect ourselves by pushing down unpleasant feelings, we also dull our ability to feel happiness and joy. A wise friend said, "If we bury one feeling, we bury them all."

In his excellent book, *The Road Less Traveled*, M. Scott Peck begins,

> Life is difficult . . . .once we truly see this truth, we transcend it. Once we truly know that life is difficult—once we truly understand and accept it—then life is no longer difficult. Because once it is accepted, the fact that life is difficult no longer matters (15).

We Can't Avoid Problems

There's no way to avoid problems. Life is full of problems, but we can learn how to solve them. This very act of struggling to understand and resolve our problems will make us stronger, more alert and alive. Peck goes on to say, "Problems call forth our courage and wisdom; indeed, they create our courage and wisdom. It is only because of problems that we grow mentally and spiritually."

So if problems are what make us grow mentally and spiritually, it doesn't seem a good idea to deny them. When we do deny them and bury the pain, we rob ourselves of vital energy, because it takes tremendous effort to keep from feeling pain. And no matter what we do, pain always wins. It demands attention and will come out, in one way or another, causing all sorts of illness, either in aberrant behavior or physical disease.

It's a paradox, I know, to stir up things that disturb our peace in the name of peace. But we're seeking a healthy peace, not a peace where conversations are on the surface and true feelings are masked and kept down. There are families and other communities that appear peaceful because voices are never raised and everything is "proper." But true feelings are not expressed and, more often than not, one person controls all the others.

Then there are other louder families or groups who may not appear peaceful at all, where everyone, down to the youngest child, has an opinion. And they all know they have the right to express it. True and honest feelings are displayed, whether it's with joy and raucous laughter or with loud, angry tears. It's all okay. And everyone, even parents, learns to say, "I'm sorry. I was wrong. Please forgive me." When parents can apologize to children, children learn a valuable lesson: it's okay to make a mistake. How wonderful to grow up knowing you don't have to be perfect, and knowing you will still be loved if you're not perfect.

Families like that are healthy families, peaceful families. Everyone can grow, because no one is afraid to be who they need to be. They know they'll find encouragement and all the help they need along this difficult road of "becoming."

Jesus was peaceful, but he certainly was not bland. He stirred things up. He got angry. He cried, he laughed, he wore no masks, and was not afraid of his human feelings. We can be that way too. Most of us are so afraid to take off our masks. *Will you still love me when you know who I really am? Will you still love me if I disagree, have my own opinions, have a different dream? Will you still love me if you know how ugly I can get, and how neurotic I can be?* Everyone feels that way. But we have to risk it. We have to be honest. There's too much at stake to try to be someone we're not. Our very lives are at stake!

The road to personal peace is not smooth. Perhaps you've been the one that's been too loud over the years and not allowed others to be honest for fear you wouldn't accept them. You may have to be a bit more quiet now and give them space to grow. Of course, this will help you to grow as well. Or perhaps you've been the quiet one, the one afraid to say what is in your heart, afraid to emerge. Maybe now is the time. And if you have to yell a little along your road to peace, then yell.

I promise you'll get there a whole lot sooner.

Prayer Keeps Us Honest

My mother was born a generation too soon. She cooked healthy meals and knew a lot about nutrition long before it became a national obsession. She didn't talk much about it; she simply prepared delicious, well-balanced meals. She didn't talk much about honesty either. She just always told the truth. And we knew it. Fortunately, almost by osmosis, we grew up knowing it was wrong to lie.

If you were fortunate to have a mother or father who taught you the value of truth, then you've probably spent most of your life living in reality, because truth is what's real. When we lie or are dishonest with others or with our own feelings, we begin to live in an unreal world. The more we try to create another world, the more we move into fantasy. And the more we live in a fantasy world, the more unstable we become. There are those unfortunate people who have never been able to escape their fantasy world, and we call them insane.

God has often been called the Ground of Reality. The more we develop our prayer life, our relationship with God, the more honest and "real" we become. I'm not comfortable with a fantasy spirituality, one that has all the answers. It's not honest. It's not real. It's phony. Give me a spirituality that lives and breathes the truth, a spirituality that doesn't have all the answers. True spirituality, real spirituality, doesn't even know all the questions! Staying grounded in God means living with Mystery. Let's get real about this. Let's get honest. We don't really know much about God. Yet we spend a lot of time trying to put God in a box. God is bigger than all our boxes, all our denominations, all our images, all our ideas about who God is.

God just is, that's all. And God loves us. Isn't that enough for us to know?

Meditation

Take some time now and reflect on your prayer life whether it has been disciplined over the years, or fleeting. It doesn't matter which. The mere fact that you are reading this book reveals that you either are or want to be a praying person.

CHAPTER FOUR

PRAYER BRINGS SURPRISES

When we pray, surprising gifts and talents emerge. For me it's been writing. It seemed as if this latent gift had been waiting all the time to surface, waiting for me to look within and notice it. I didn't grow up saying I wanted to be a writer. I never even tried to write until after I started praying, and I didn't get published until I was forty-two years old. Writing came as a tremendous shock to me. When I walk through a book store and see my books on a shelf, I'm still amazed.

It started after I had been praying for a few years. I began to have humorous thoughts about my mother-in-law, of the many funny things she would say and do. I went around laughing to myself—for days—until it occurred to me that maybe I was supposed to write these things down. So I did, and it resulted in my first published piece (which I shared with you in Chapter Three).

After that I became obsessed with writing. Once I saw my name in print, I was hooked! But I didn't know what in the world I was doing. I thought getting that article published so easily might just have been some sort of dumb luck. I had so many doubts and a lot of negative self-talk. "Judy, you're over forty. Remember? You're going to start writing now? You don't know the first thing about it. You don't even know any writers. You were just lucky." But the thoughts kept coming—ideas for novels, ideas for articles, ideas for columns. I knew I was supposed to write.

Several years ago, journalist Bill Moyers conducted a series of interviews with Joseph Campbell, the great mythologist. Campbell often said, "Follow your bliss." He also said, to paraphrase, when you follow your bliss, the whole universe will cooperate. Doors will open. You'll meet just the right people at just the right time. It's as if an invisible hand is guiding you.

That is exactly what happened to me. I started meeting writers. I met Og Mandino, the famous motivational author whose first book (written decades ago when Og was 42!) is still selling around the world today. Millions of copies of *The Greatest Salesman in the World* have sold, making it the all-time best-seller of any motivational book in history! I actually met him, and he loved my writing and wrote testimonies for my books. I don't think this was an accident.

I met other writers, too, who gave me practical help. They led me to the right books on writing, gave me tips on publishing, advised me on how to write query letters and prepare manuscripts using the proper format. Someone finally told me what a SASE was! (a self-addressed stamped envelope, in case you were wondering too).

Then I remember Eddie Ensley holding up his palm and saying, "The rules of writing can be counted on one hand." Was that all there was to it? I could learn a few rules. I thought I had to read all the classic literature, know who all the great writers were, have an English or Journalism degree. I thought I had to have credentials! But no one asked me for any.

I did, however, have to work hard at my writing. And I had to keep believing that God really did give me this gift. Eventually I grew confident and knew I had a responsibility to cultivate my talent and use it well. During the first few years of writing, I had a strong feeling of being "led." Every time I had a question, the answer would come. And before I knew it I had more articles published in the national Catholic press. Then my first book. What a thrill! Then the second, the third, and now the fourth. Joseph Campbell was right. When I followed my inner guide, and did what made me truly happy, the universe opened before me.

After my books were published, I started getting invitations to speak at churches and to women's groups. This was another whole new adventure and a scary one. Again I met the right people, other speakers. The right information and teaching tools came my way. I learned how to write and deliver inspiring speeches. Me! A person who had been scared to death to stand up in front of people.

So when we give ourselves to God and begin to pray deeply, life may take us in new and wonderful directions. But if the thought of that makes you nervous, know that God won't make you go where you don't want to go, but will allow you to go where you truly do want to go.

No matter how old or how young you are, if there's something you're just longing to do, something blissful, go ahead and take that first step. And watch in wonder as the universe opens wide—just for you. We all have different gifts. Whatever your gift is, it will be uniquely yours. Maybe you have a special gift for working with children, or the elderly, or people with disabilities. Or maybe you're a tremendous listener.

My husband has a rare and much-needed gift. He's a peacemaker. He has an uncanny ability to help people settle their differences, often in extremely difficult circumstances. He can go into a group of angry people who are arguing and out of control, and he brings peace. He has this gentle way about him. He listens to all sides and helps people to step back and see the situation from another's viewpoint. And somehow everyone comes away feeling they've won. I can't tell you how often he's done that, in family situations, at work, in parish council meetings. Would you find it surprising if I told you his favorite prayer for years has been the St. Francis peace prayer? I think we become what we want to become.

So if you have a little inkling that seems a bit crazy, don't push it aside. Think about it. Pray about it. Then watch the doors open. And when the time is right (and you'll know when it is), offer your gift in loving service to a needy, waiting world.

That's who the gift is really for.

Prayer Helps Us Let Go

There is an appointed time for everything,
     and a time for every affair under the heavens.
A time to be born, and a time to die;
A time to plant, and a time to uproot the plant.
A time to kill, and a time to heal;
A time to tear down, and a time to build,
A time to weep, and a time to laugh;
A time to mourn, and a time to dance (Eccl 3:1-4).

Letting go has a lot to do with timing. There is a time to raise children, and a time to let them go. A time to be newborn Christians, and a time to mature. A time to be young, and a time to grow old. A time to feel pain, and a time for it to subside. A time to feel ecstatic joy, and a time to be content without it. It's all in the timing.

For me, letting go meant I had to learn how to get in step, because I was forever lagging behind. I wrote my third book, _Letting Go_, because I was so incredibly out of step. I was approaching my 50th birthday, and everything was changing. Our children were leaving, and I was going through all those conflicting feelings. Some days I'd think, "Oh, I can't wait until they all leave; they're driving me crazy" (mostly during the teen years). And there were other times when I would say, "Oh, I hope they don't leave too soon. I wish they wouldn't grow up so fast."

Other more subtle changes were taking place. My hair was getting gray, and my body was yielding to gravity. I'd look in the mirror and think, just a little tuck around my eyes, and maybe under my neck. It wouldn't take much. I was having problems. Time was marching on, but I couldn't go forward. I was stuck. I didn't want to let go of so many things.

So I wrote about all the things I knew I had to let go of, and somehow in the writing, and in the reflection about my life, I was able to move on. I was able, finally, to get in step. Why is letting go so important? The following "Spring Cleaning" reflection from my book *Letting Go* may offer some insight:

My heart is cluttered, God. And so are my "special" drawers and boxes and little hiding places. They're bulging with letters and pictures and "things" that hold lovely, bittersweet memories.

How can I let the treasure of my life go? Can I just whisk it all up in my arms and throw it into the trash? I can't let it go. These things are too precious to me. Yet, I know I must do something. I must make way for the "now," for the present-day experience that will soon enough be tomorrow's memory.

How often I find myself looking at the wave long after it has passed me when the new wave takes me by surprise. I didn't see it coming. I was still remembering and yearning for the last experience, the best wave, or so I thought. But each wave you bring me, God, is the best wave. Each one is fresh and exhilarating.

I'm trying, you know I am, to experience life as a fantastic piece of music. I don't want to stay too long with a note that's meant to be a staccato, even when it jabs my soul and makes me bleed. I need to move on with the music and flow and dance with it. But you know how I tend to linger too long, not trusting that the next measure will touch and embrace me as much as the last.

Help me, God, to unclutter my heart. Give me a thorough spring cleaning and rearrange me any way you like. How I need fresh air and room to breathe. I want to be empty so I can feel the new wave washing over me. I want to be refreshed and ready to listen with my whole heart to the new song filling my soul.

Letting go is important because we need "fresh air and room to breathe." We need to be emptied out, cleansed, so we can experience the present moment, the now. Then we will feel the new wave washing over us. We will listen with our whole heart to the new song God is singing to us, and we will flow with life.

Life is meant to be a beautiful, graceful dance. But we'll only know that if we let God lead us. And when it's a slow dance, we'll want to embrace our partner. But how can we if our arms are full? There are times in life when we simply need to throw caution to the wind, drop everything, and take to dancing.

Positive Experiences

For me the positive experiences of my life have been the most difficult to let go of. I'm like a "peak experience" junkie. For example, I didn't really know true joy until I got married and started having children. I didn't conceive easily; it took five years each time. So I loved being pregnant and having babies. I had such an appreciation for the whole experience, because I longed for each of our three children for so many years.

Each time I gave birth, I would relive it in my mind over and over. I'd picture myself back in the delivery room, see the doctor hold up the baby, remember exactly how this new miracle sounded. Was there one little cry, or two, or did the baby wail? I remembered when the nurse put the newborn on my chest, and that first look, baby's eyes looking right into mine. It was pure, magical, joy.

And the years when the kids were little were so precious. I'd recall their first steps, their first words, and their first day at kindergarten. And then all the birthdays, first communions, and even the awful days when each of them drove off in the family car for the first time, with me in the passenger seat! The memories were my treasure, and I held them tightly in my heart, not wanting time to steal them away.

After a while, I simply had to move on. I knew the reason I was reluctant was that those years and all those experiences were precious. And I wanted them to be safe. Then it came to me that they were also precious to God, and would never be lost. God doesn't forget. God is like a mother and treasures our lives too. God so treasures us that whatever is important to us is important to God. And who but God could truly appreciate the sacredness of it all anyway? When I believed and trusted that every precious detail of my life would always be remembered, I finally moved on. But it took time.

I was like a trapeze artist, swinging back and forth, back and forth, trying to gain courage. God swung the bar out to me many times; I was too frightened to reach for it. But then one day I just couldn't think about it anymore. I simply let go and stretched out my arms, reaching for the golden bar growing more beautiful as it moved towards me. I had to trust God, and trust the timing.

It was a terrifying moment, letting go of the familiar bar—my life—while reaching for the next. And for a split second, I felt like I was floundering in mid-air. Snatches of my childhood, fleeting images and old familiar feelings, colors, and even smells from every stage of my life floated all around me. I didn't try to catch them. I just kissed them goodbye, at least for a little while, and whispered, "Until we meet again."

And the next thing I knew, I caught the bar. Amazing! Suddenly I was there. I was really there, in a new place, a larger place. It was peaceful. And there was a tenderness in the air. I felt as if I had swung right into God's arms, and God was pleased.

That's a rather poetic way of putting it, but perhaps we think our world will get smaller if we let go. We wonder what will fill our lives once they have been emptied. Ah, but that's where the excitement begins. God surprises us, uses us in different ways, helps us see new talents and new directions we can pursue.

But first we have to entrust the treasures of our lives to God and then move into the future. We simply cannot make progress in prayer when we're stuck in the past. So let go, when you're ready, and reach for the bar. Remember, it's all in the timing. Take a deep breath now…

Prayer Makes Us Adventurers

I've always had a yen to explore, to go to exotic places I've never been. I haven't traveled extensively yet, but this craving has been satisfied through years of "soul travel." I had no idea, not even the slightest inkling, it would be such an adventure. Committing to a life of prayer is like jumping on a train without asking where it's going. You don't even care about the destination. You're on a high adventure of the heart—the adventure of "becoming." Leo Buscaglia ("the hug doctor") says, "Once you are involved in the process of becoming, there is no stopping. You're doomed! You're gone! But what a fantastic journey."

That's what happened to me. I was doomed. I'm still doomed. There's no stopping, no turning back. The "adventure train" slowed down for me that fateful weekend nearly twenty years ago, and I've never regretted for a moment that I hopped on without asking one single question. I didn't know where I was going then, and I don't know where I'm going now, but I do know who's taking me!

The adventure train is not always smooth riding. Sometimes it travels through dark tunnels before ascending the mountain pass where the view is breathtaking. And you wonder, with trepidation and excitement, what's on the other side of that blind curve? You'll just have to trust, and wait for the treasure that is yours right around the bend. Or you may have to hold on with all your might as you plummet down the mountainside and back through another dark tunnel. It's all part of the ride that will take you into your own deep life.

Prayer has to do with becoming who you are supposed to become. It has to do with becoming all that you can be. You may not understand all the ups and downs of the ride, because spiritual development is such a long journey. It requires patience and most of all trust. For the person who prays, one thing is sure. You'll never be bored! Soul travel, the journey into one's own soul, is the greatest adventure in the world. So hold on—with white knuckles if you must—you're in for the ride of your life!

Prayer Moves Us Beyond Ourselves

Have you ever found yourself saying something you didn't plan to say? I don't mean the times you stuck your foot in your mouth. We all do that occasionally. I mean the times you said precisely the right thing. It just came rolling off your tongue. And did you ever do something that, up until the time you did it, you thought there's no way you had the strength or even the will to do it?

Our oldest daughter is married, and she and her husband have blessed us with three gorgeous granddaughters. René and I are best of friends, now. But when she was a teenager... Recently one of her daughters was giving her a hard time, and she looked at me and said, "You're enjoying this, aren't you, Mom?" I just smiled, answering, "I'm waiting until she's a teenager." (Please God, let me live that long.)

I'll never forget one day when René was about sixteen. We were in the middle of a heated argument about who knows what. Both of our Italian mouths were going a hundred miles an hour when suddenly, in a flash, I saw her as my little three-year-old. A strong protective motherly instinct came over me. No one was going to hurt my baby, not even me. I found myself putting my arms around her—just like that—in the middle of an argument. I told her I loved her and that I was sorry. The instant I moved to put my arms around her, I felt a surge of love come through me. I know she felt it too.

This happened shortly after I had started to pray deeply. God began to change me almost immediately, and my daughter and I got along better after that. Of course we had to work on our relationship, but I had so much help now. I could understand her better. God gave me little insights, valuable flashes into her personality and, of course, my own.

I survived two more teenagers after that, with a lot less anxiety and conflict, because I had more years of praying and growing in by that time. When I'm with young mothers, I advise them to start praying now, no matter how hard it is to find quiet time. I tell them to take turns watching one another's children, whatever it takes, so they can develop their relationship with God now. I was a much better mother after I started to pray. I was a happier mother, and I think that's a tremendous gift to children.

Another incident comes to mind. I was arguing (again) with a man who was part of a group we prayed with. (You've noticed I like to argue. I could try to blame that on my Italian genes, too.) But we had a strong "disagreement" about a spiritual matter, and I was clearly right and he was clearly wrong. I was pretty darn ticked off and acting arrogant and pompous when suddenly I actually heard the most loving, kind voice say, "Humility, my child." I didn't hear the voice in my ears, weird as that sounds. I heard it in my mouth, around my tongue, which has always been my worst enemy.

I immediately calmed down, rather stunned, and listened to the point the man was trying to make. He was still clearly wrong, but I had learned one of the best lessons of my life. Being loving is better than being right. Over the years, this type of experience has played itself out in my life in dozens of situations. I have never heard that loving voice again, but I've found myself saying and doing things I never could have thought of on my own.

So change is not a grinding, arduous kind of thing when we pray. It happens naturally when we submit ourselves to God's will. We act in ways we've always wanted to act but didn't know how to push past our own boundaries. All we have to do is listen to our Inner Guide, trust our intuitions, and take the first step. God will do the rest.

I had a dream about this once. I was standing high up on a ladder about to walk across a tightrope. I was scared to death and stood frozen for some time. But I knew God was on the other side waiting for me. Finally, slowly, I moved one foot out. The moment my toes touched the rope, I found myself gliding all the way across—swiftly, effortlessly. When I awoke, the message was clear. All I had to do was take the first step. That's all God requires of us, our willingness to change, and some small sign of action.

How much easier could God make it for us? When we under-

stand how God works, what possible excuse could we have for
not changing?

Prayer Makes Us More Like God

Isn't it strange how people who have been married a long time
seem to look alike? They don't really, yet they do. It's difficult to
explain, but if you've seen it you know what I mean.

This is what happens to people who pray. The more time we
spend with God, the more we become like God. When we read
Scripture regularly, we take on the "mind of Christ." We start
applying Christlike attitudes and values to everyday life.
Eventually God can be seen in one who prays. It happens slowly—and usually without conscious awareness. As the following
Scripture passage reveals, it happens when we remove our many
veils or masks. "All of us, gazing on the Lord's glory with
unveiled faces, are being transformed from glory to glory into his
very image by the Lord who is the Spirit" (2 Cor 3:18).

I remember seeing a woman perusing items in a religious gift
shop one day. I didn't know her personally at the time; I just
knew of her. She was a woman of deep prayer who would soon
become my spiritual director. I was struck by the look on her face.
She was completely at peace. As I moved closer to the counter
where she was standing, I felt a quiet sense of well-being and
comfort. She emanated God! And I felt so fortunate to be standing near her.

Prayer is powerful. God fills to overflowing those who pray,
and by their very presence they become healers. That woman did-
n't even know I was there. She didn't know that she was gifting
me with the fruit of her prayer.

Another time I was standing in a checkout line at the grocery
store. There was a young man in front of me who appeared to be
in his late twenties. He wasn't especially handsome or tall or
muscular. But there was something beautiful about him. He was
simply paying for his groceries, but that same grace, or spiritual
essence, or whatever you want to call it, was flowing from him. I
saw him on another occasion and again I felt the same sweetness.

This is a mysterious thing and difficult to describe. It's not the same as being in the presence of someone who has a good personality or striking good looks, or someone who is gregarious and delightful to be around. It's different. The people I'm talking about are almost transparent, and something invisible and healing gently radiates from them to the world. They are conduits of God.

I discovered this wonderful passage in *The Cloud of Unknowing* that explains it so well:

> As a person matures in the work of love, he [sic] will discover that this love governs his demeanor befittingly both within and without. When grace draws a man to contemplation it seems to transfigure him even physically so that though he may be ill-favored by nature, he now appears changed and lovely to behold. His whole personality becomes so attractive that good people are honored and delighted to be in his company, strengthened by the sense of God he radiates (117).

Prayer takes on new meaning here. We have this magnificent opportunity to carry God to the world! Maybe this, and this alone, can be one's gift, just living and mingling with people in our daily lives, letting God touch them through us.

Prayer Helps Slow Time Down

How often we find ourselves saying (especially at the end of the year), "Where on earth did the time go?"

We all wish we could slow time down. One of the great benefits of prayer is that it helps us do just that. It has something to do with the rhythm—the coming back again and again to our prayer. Ideally, it will be morning and evening, but even if it's once a day, or three or four times a week, it's the regular, sustained discipline that does it. And if we couple our prayer with keeping a journal, we somehow get more control of the events of our lives. We take time to reflect on the birthdays, marriages, births, deaths, conversions, passages. We take into prayer what we're learning, how we feel, how we've made connections with our earthly and spiritual heritage.

The practice of prayer forces us to stop and dwell for a while in our own precious life instead of racing through life day after day, year after year, until suddenly we're old. I don't mind that I'm growing older now, because I've prayed deeply for nearly twenty years. Consequently, I've "lived" deeply. I've reflected and written about all the significant events of my life. In my journal, I've recorded dreams and memories, how my relationships were developing, arguments (plenty of those), stories of forgiveness, healings, insights into how to become a better person, and on and on.

"Our days are like those of grass; like a flower of the field we bloom. The wind sweeps over us and we are gone, and our place knows us no more" (Ps 103:15–16). When I first read these words, they frightened me. My biggest fear was that I would come to the end of my life feeling like I had never truly lived. I wasn't concerned about the wind sweeping over me and being gone. I was afraid it would happen before I had a chance to bloom.

The starkness of this psalm has stayed with me through the years. The image of blossoming is always somewhere in my mind, and I know it's related to prayer. Prayer is what helps us recognize our gifts and talents in the first place. And prayer is what helps us bloom. This takes time. We can't let time slip away if we want to flower. We need to grab onto it and slow it down so we can learn how to live deeply.

If you say, "But I don't have time for prayer," my answer is, you will when you start to pray. I know it sounds crazy, but if you start praying, your time will multiply and you'll have no idea how it happened. You can't outdo God. You'll discover you're more productive than you've ever been when you commit yourself to daily prayer.

When I started to write this book, I didn't know how I would get it done. I still work full time, so naturally when I get home at night I'm tired. And as much as I love writing, after working at a computer all day long it's pretty difficult to come home and work at a computer at night. Even before I started the book, I felt that I didn't have enough time for everything in my life.

So what did I decide to do about it? Pray more. I started getting up earlier in the morning to increase my time for prayer and Scripture reading. Then I added more time to my evening contemplative prayer. The results have been remarkable. I've had more energy, have been calmer and more peaceful, and I have also had more time! The more you pray, the more God will slow time down for you. If someone had told me this years ago I wouldn't have believed it. So if you're skeptical, I understand. But I challenge you to try it for two weeks and see for yourself.

"Give, and it shall be given to you. Good measure pressed down, shaken together, running over, will they pour into the fold of your garment. For the measure you measure with will be measured back to you" (Lk 6:38).

Prayer Calms the Whirlwind

Many people live in a whirlwind and postpone their hopes and dreams, waiting for the winds to die down. Then, when things are more settled, they tell themselves, I'll think about God.

I'll never forget the words I saw printed on a card years ago. "This is the urgency. Live! And have your blooming in the noise of the whirlwind." We can't wait until our lives are calm, our children grown, our debts paid, our addictions cured, our relationships mended, to develop spiritually. _Now_ is the time. In the midst of the frightening whirlwind.

It's good to remember that whirlwinds are only hot air. They come and go and usually just blow themselves out. It is possible to be calm, to grow, and to be transformed in spite of the stormy weather that often typifies our lives. If, that is, we pray. I have to pray, every day. When I don't, the whirlwinds begin to scare me. I forget they're just hot air. So we need God to remind us that today's roaring whirlwind will be a mere whimper tomorrow. We need God to speak to us in the midst of our busyness and anxieties. And if we are to hear God with all that noise going on, we may have to rethink our lives and the various roles we play.

We may even have to raise our hand, like Jesus did, and calm the storm. There's no reason why we can't say, "Enough. I can't do this anymore. I've allowed my life to get out of control, to become unmanageable, confused. This has to stop. Enough."

It's your life, so what's stopping you? Take command....

Prayer Exercise

In the space provided below, or on a separate piece of paper, answer these questions after reflecting on them prayerfully:

1. How has the practice of prayer changed you?

2. What gift or talent has emerged that has taken you by surprise?

3. What "thorn in your side" have you learned to live with?

_____

_____

_____

_____

_____

_____

_____

_____

CHAPTER FIVE

MAKING ROOM
FOR PRAYER

After my encounter with God, I took a good, long look at my life and decided I had to make some changes. I just couldn't keep doing everything myself. Super Woman, Suzie Homemaker, and Perfect Mother were ruining my life. And though you would think they were wonderful for my family, they were doing them in as well. The situation wasn't healthy for anyone. Mostly it was my fault, because I wanted to control everything. And it was driving me crazy because I couldn't.

One of the first "blessed" moments after my conversion came with this insight: I had to give up control. So I called a family meeting and said, "Okay, kids—you're going to do this, you're going to do that, you're going to do this. Mom can't keep doing everything herself anymore. I need help."

Much to my surprise, they all got right into it. They even liked it! Together we made "chore" lists. They learned how to cook and clean. And though some of my friends were appalled, I even taught my children how to sort their clothes and wash them. How hard is it to throw clothes into an automatic washer and dryer? I did my best to ignore comments like, "You can't be serious. You make your kids wash their own clothes?" It wasn't as though they had to do it on a scrub board! I didn't say, "Here, kids, take these clothes down to the river and find a rock!"

I was on the road back to sanity, and if it meant I had to put up with a little criticism, so be it. The kids were becoming more confident because they were learning new skills, and I felt less pressured. Things were working! It was wonderful not having to do everything myself. One way my husband helped was by doing a lot of the cooking. And he had the nerve to get better than me! People started raving about his wonderful Italian cooking! Unfortunately, when you give up control and start delegating, you also give up some of the praise. There's a lot of strokes that come when you keep a nice house and make good meals and desserts. But I've learned to live without those strokes, and quite nicely too. But when Rick's getting all the applause, I still can't resist saying, "I taught him everything he knows." (He has a way of forgetting that!)

The reason I was trying to get my life in better order and balance was so I could make time for daily prayer. It was hard at first because the kids were still young. I asked Rick to help me. I said, "I'm going to go into our room every day and shut the door and pray. Please, please keep the kids away." And he was very supportive and understanding. I could hear him telling the kids, "Leave Mom alone. She's praying. She'll be out in a little bit."

But they couldn't stand to see the door closed, and they would find every excuse in the world to come in. "Mom, I need the shampoo, right now. We're out in our bathroom." "Mom, I need to tell you something really, really, really important." "Mom, Ricky hit me."

Finally, I took them aside and said, "Kids, Mom's going to pray every single day. When you see that door closed, don't come near it. Don't knock on that door unless someone's bleeding... and it had better be a lot of blood."

After a while they got used to it. Even now when they come over they'll say, "Where's Mom?" Someone will answer, "She's praying. She'll be out in a little bit." They're not ashamed to say "Mom's praying." They grew up with it.

So, how do we fit prayer into our busy lives? How do we make it a priority? We *make* it a priority. And when we do, everything else seems to fall into place. It doesn't make sense, but somehow when we give God time every day, we're able to do more than we did before. This amazed me at first. God was giving me more time in direct proportion to how much time I spent in prayer.

I found myself working more productively. I'd get things done in half the time it used to take me. When I was faithful to prayer, I'd move through the day a little more slowly, really "living" it, yet at nightfall I found I had accomplished more than I ever was able to in the past.

Maybe it's been a while since you've taken a good look at your life. What can you let go of? Who's holding you back? Super Woman? Perfect Person? Volunteer of the Year (maybe the decade)?

I had gotten lost in all my roles. I didn't know who I was until I started to pray. Don't get lost in busyness. God wants to spend time with the real you and wants you to spend time with the real you too.

Sorting Things Out

When we become serious about prayer and allow God to move more freely in our lives, we begin to sort things out. Little by little we rid ourselves of clutter. Somehow we know what to drop and what to keep. Is this committee or project or hobby really what I'm supposed to be doing? Is it even what I want to be doing? After prayer and discernment we find the courage to quit, say no, take a leave of absence, or whatever we need to simplify our lives.

We may stay with some things, but we'll be able to work much better when we're not so scattered. When God directs our "comings and goings"—our work, our hobbies, our education, our ministries—we stay in balance. So often people who are newly converted think they have to go out and save the world. They say yes to everything that comes along, and before they know it they're burned out. I know, because it happened to me. But it only happened once. I said, "But God, how could this be? Here I've been doing all these good things, for you, and look at me, I can hardly move."

You're probably smiling by now. Maybe you've been there. I think it's called the "Messiah Complex." It was such a relief to understand (God showed me when I was lying on the bed so fatigued even my bones ached) that God could handle the job just fine. God never asked me to do all those things. I never really asked God what I should be doing. I just said, yes, yes, yes. But now I say no, no, no, without the slightest twinge of guilt, and only say yes when I know God is leading me in a certain direction.

Our first and most important calling is right in our own homes, building the best relationships we can with our spouses, our children, our friends, our religious communities, or wherever and with whomever we're planted. Too often all the busyness, the good things we're doing to "help" God, is really escapism. It's too hard to learn how to communicate, to forgive and ask forgiveness, to teach our children how to love. It's easier to go out and do our "good work."

Of course I don't mean to diminish all the work that needs to be done in the world. We all need to do something, and we need to teach our children how to serve others through our good example. But we don't need to do everything! And if we start with building healthy relationships and peaceful homes, we've done extremely important work that will make the world a better place. If our children know they are loved beyond measure, think of the good we've done. Sending healthy, self-confident children into the world is far more important than any committee work.

Yes, it's harder. I know it is. But I'm convinced that God wants us to start there. So take a deep breath and try this. Say "no." Say it again, only louder. You don't have to cover your head. The

world won't cave in. Practice it. "No, no, no, no, no."
Tell the truth now, doesn't it feel wonderful?

Prayer Exercise

Take some time now to reflect on your daily life. Are you constantly on the run? Does the thought of sitting down every day to pray seem impossible to you? If so, make a list of your activities (not the essential ones like work, caring for family, exercise, or school). Spend some time with the list. What are you doing that you really don't want to be doing? Maybe you were "guilted" into it. Maybe you just couldn't say no at the time. Go through the list quietly and prayerfully. Ask God to help you simplify your life so you'll have time to develop spiritually.

Take a second sheet of paper now, and list only those activities you feel are important, that you *want* to do, and that you feel God is asking you to do. It may take time to balance your life, so don't feel as if you have to drop out of everything tomorrow. But this simple exercise of putting it all down on paper and asking God to direct your "comings and goings" will set things in motion. And before you know it, you'll be back in control of your time... and your life.

CHAPTER SIX

THE CALL TO PRAYER

How does one move deeper into prayer? Do you just decide one day you're going to become a contemplative? Do you read about it first? Do you study the writings of the great spiritual fathers and mothers of the church?

Or are you called…

The author of *The Cloud of Unknowing* states, "Contemplation is not the fruit of study but a gift of grace" (98). This gift is not usually given in the beginning, right after we're awakened. We're too keyed up, too excited. Rather than being quiet, we're more likely to want to shout a little. God is real! Hallelujah!

We do have a strong desire to pray, however, and we begin in whatever way we're comfortable. For Catholics, the rosary may become very important, or other traditional prayers of the church. When I started praying I used everything. I had a stack of little devotional booklets, two or three rosaries, the Liturgy of the Hours, which I could never figure out how to use but loved (still do) the inspiring non-biblical readings in the back of the book by great saints who lived hundreds of years ago.

I crammed it all in, along with my personal litany of "worry prayers" for my children. That was always long, repetitious, and somewhat frantic. Then I prayed for everyone and everything else. I guess my prayer time was good (it certainly was long), but it was also exhausting. After a while it became such a chore. I started forgetting some of the people and some of the things I was "supposed" to be praying for. Some days I'd sit down in my prayer chair and I could hardly speak a word. I honestly thought my prayer life was falling apart.

This is the first sign that God is inviting us to go deeper, perhaps into contemplative prayer, and at first we're confused. We may even feel guilty. But what if I don't say my rosary, or complete this devotional prayer book? And, oh no, I forgot to pray for my children today!

But when God calls us to the quiet, we don't have a taste for our earlier ways of praying, except occasionally. And it's okay to go back and forth for a while. But we're being asked to let go, to follow God into silence. When I sensed that this was true for me, I started reading a little here and there about contemplative prayer. I had no idea what it was; I even had a hard time pronouncing the word. But the strangest thing occurred. Almost from the first time I saw the words "contemplative prayer" in print, I had a strong interest in it.

One day I received a flyer in the mail. There was going to be a contemplative prayer retreat in town. I have no idea how that flyer found its way to my mailbox. We had just moved from Ohio to Phoenix, Arizona, where Rick had been transferred to a new position. We had barely been to Mass at our new church—I don't think we had even registered yet. And the retreat wasn't even being held at our church, but at another one clear across town. But here was this flyer, addressed to me. Who even knew my address?

Eagerly, I read every word and quickly called the number listed at the bottom of the form to register. It was to be conducted by

Contemplative Brothers, Eddie Ensley and Robert Herrmann. I'd never heard of them and had never seen any retreat billed as "contemplative." But my heart started to beat a little faster. I went to the bedroom and marked my calendar. A whole month away. I wished it were tomorrow.

The weeks dragged. I thought about the upcoming contemplative retreat constantly. I anticipated it like I used to anticipate Christmas when I was a child. I really didn't know why I felt that way, but I simply could not wait for the day to come.

"Contemplative Brothers"

Finally, I was there. It was a Friday evening, and Eddie Ensley was at the podium giving his opening remarks. He was stocky, wore glasses, and appeared to be in his early thirties. I can't remember what he said, but I liked him. He was warm and funny and spoke with a southern drawl.

Robert Herrmann was sitting in the first pew. I was really curious about him—he was so young! Only twenty-one I found out later. He had light brown, shoulder-length hair. His high cheekbones hinted at his Cherokee heritage. I watched him as he watched Eddie, still speaking. Robert was attentive, smiling and nodding, looking back at the audience from time to time with a gentle look of love in his eyes.

Then he got up to speak. He took his time, looking around slowly at the group, from face to face, and said softly, "I've been thinking about you for months, praying for you, wondering about you. Wondering who you were, what your life was like, how you might look. I started praying for you and sending my love to you long ago, to each one of you that God would call."

Was that the pull I felt? Had God used this young man to call me here? Little did I know at that moment what an important part of my life Robert Herrmann would become. I don't remember anything else Robert said in that opening talk, but there was something about both of these men that captured my heart. I later discovered that many people who attended that retreat felt the same way. Eddie and Robert had spent countless hours in prayer, preparing for the retreats they were giving in California and Arizona. Robert told me later that he had spent as many as six to eight hours a day in contemplative prayer. As I watched (and experienced) Robert and Eddie that weekend, I had the first glimpse of how powerful this kind of prayer could be.

Throughout the weekend they alternated giving talks. Eddie was a church history scholar and theologian. He unearthed the rich tradition of the Catholic church, telling colorful stories of great saints, reciting from ancient texts that moved me deeply. He made me feel connected to the first Christians, and that I truly belonged in this long line of people God calls from generation to generation.

Eddie's talks were laced with humor and interesting facts as he traced a history of the church. He also led the group in guided meditations using rich imagery and soothing background music. Step by step, he taught us how to pray.

Robert talked about his own journey, and how the practice of contemplative prayer had transformed him. He told of a dream he had where he was dressed in a monk's habit, speaking to a large group of people, and how he had been scared to death to get up in front of people to speak. But then he found himself, not in a dream this time, at the age of twenty, leading a day's retreat for the priests, religious sisters, and religious brothers of the Archdiocese of Los Angeles.

Eddie then told of how he had given a tape to a well-known Jesuit priest and spiritual writer. On the tape, Robert described his prayer life. The priest was deeply moved and shared it with other religious leaders. They all agreed that Robert was a person with great intuitive wisdom about prayer, a person who had developed a prayer life of rare depth. They wanted to meet him and learn more, so they invited him to lead them in a day-long retreat.

I was fascinated by all of this. I sat leaning forward in the front row throughout the weekend and hung on their every word. Early into the retreat I began to have what could only be called a mystical experience. It had to do with Robert. Because of some special grace, or because he had spent so much time in prayer, he seemed to be absolutely transparent. I had the uncanny feeling I was looking at Jesus. It wasn't anything he was saying—it was just him. His very presence was healing me.

Sharing the Experience

At the end of the retreat, on Sunday afternoon, Eddie and Robert asked if anyone would like to share their experience of the weekend. I was shocked when one person after another stood up to say that every time they looked at Robert, they felt as if they were looking at Jesus. I was afraid to say that, or to even tell anyone of my experience. How could it be? I knew I was looking at a very holy young man, but he was human! How could I explain to anyone that I could see Jesus?

This wasn't like looking at a saintly person. It was different. I could "see" past Robert to the Divine Presence dwelling within him. It was almost like Robert wasn't really there, but someone else was looking at me through his deep green eyes. People were speaking, stumbling around, attempting to articulate what I'm trying to say here. And I hadn't told anyone what had been happening to me. I thought they'd laugh, or think I was some sort of religious fanatic. But now it was clear—something holy and mysterious was going on in this place.

Finally, I did get up to speak. I said I, too, was having the same experience. I told how I had anticipated attending this retreat, and how strange it was since I didn't know a thing about contemplative prayer. I made a few more comments, lingering a little, not wanting the weekend to end. While I was speaking, I didn't notice that Robert had quietly come down from the platform. And as I turned to go back to my seat I stopped dead in my tracks. Robert was standing there, right in front of me, with his arms outstretched. He might as well have had a long, white robe and sandals on, because the person who embraced me was Christ himself. I felt surrounded by a mild electricity that was filled with love. It was the same healing vibration I had felt in my kitchen years before that rescued me from despair. Finally, I said, "Thank you, Jesus... I mean, Robert."

The audience laughed and so did we. They knew I was half-kidding but they understood, because it seemed we were having a "group" mystical experience. We could all see the Lord, and none of us knew what to make of it. I went back to my seat, a little dazed, and wondered how on earth I could ever go back to ordinary life.

The Gift of Tears
The next morning I awoke filled with the most awful pain in my heart, with a love I could not endure. St. Thérèse, the Little Flower, wrote about being pierced with love. That's what it felt like, like someone had pierced my heart. Rick was getting ready for work, and I had to get the kids up for school. Fortunately, it was one of the few periods in my life that I wasn't working since we had recently moved.

I managed to hold back the tears until everyone was out of the house. Then they came, from some deep, deep place inside of me, like a flood. Oddly, they were neither tears of sadness nor tears of joy. I can't explain what they were. It was just this painful feeling of love. I cried for three days. Rick was worried about me, and I kept saying, "It's okay. I'm all right. God is doing something to me."

These were not ordinary tears but healing tears, deep, down to my core. One eastern Spiritual Father is quoted in the inspiring book *In Search of True Wisdom*: "Lamentations are an overflowing tenderness of heart united with the sorrow of a humble and penitential heart. These tears proceed from the depths of the heart and envelop the soul." I did feel enveloped, for hours and days. On the third day, I was standing in the living room all alone, still filled with loving pain and tears. I couldn't take it anymore. I cried out loud, "God, what are you doing to me? Are you trying to kill me with your love?"

Before the contemplative retreat I had been reading a book titled *My Other Self* by Clarence Enzler. I noticed it now on the coffee table, and for some reason I snatched it up and it fell open. My eyes were riveted to these words: "You are being readied for contemplative prayer." It was all I saw on the page. It was as if those words were highlighted in bright yellow, and the rest of the page was in the darkened background. My knees grew weak as I lowered myself down to the couch. "You are being readied for contemplative prayer." This was all God's plan, from the moment the flyer came in the mail. That's why I had been so drawn to the retreat. That's why I had the experience with Robert. That's why I was crying these healing tears. I was being prepared for contemplative prayer.

Little by little the pain subsided and the tears dried up. I found that as I expressed the overflowing love that was "killing" me, I felt better. Several nights later we met with a group of friends at church and they looked so different to me. I felt a new compassion and total acceptance, for them and for me. We were who we were, right then. With all of our faults, all of our struggles, all of our inherited and acquired disabilities and flaws. We just were. And all of it was okay.

"First pray for the gift of tears, so that through sorrowing you may tame what is savage in your soul" (*Philokalia* 58, see Resources on page 105). There was nothing savage left in me. And what a miracle that was. The gift of tears was not an ending to a perfectly beautiful story. It was the beginning, an invitation to go deeper, to a place of stillness, a place I knew little about.

"Be Still and Know that I Am God"

Silence—sweet, scary silence. We want it. We don't want it. We crave it, but we're afraid of it. Silence makes us nervous. Lulls in conversation are quickly filled with idle, nonsensical chatter. Talk about the weather, tell a corny joke, say something. Anything! Anything is better than silence. But silence is where "it" happens. Silence is where we learn about ourselves. Silence is where we find God.

Spending even ten or fifteen minutes once or twice a day, just sitting quietly, sinking into silence, will change your life forever. This focused concentration will spill over into all areas of your life and move you to a place of peace, creativity, and inner healing.

There are many books on prayer that I highly recommend—from the Christian classics such as *Interior Castle*, the writings of St. Teresa of Avila; *Dark Night of the Soul*, by St. John of the Cross; *The Cloud of Unknowing*; to more contemporary books like *Open Mind, Open Heart* by Thomas Keating; *Dance of the Spirit*, by Maria Harris; and *Prayer That Heals Our Emotions*, by my friend Eddie Ensley. But you don't have to read them all before you begin to pray this way. You just begin, a little each day. And you learn along the way.

You can keep your devotionals, rosaries, Jesus beads, and prayer books nearby. There will be times when you'll just want the comfort of them. Simply holding them in your lap, or fingering your beads, will help you bridge the gap into silence. You may find yourself going back and forth for a while, and that's all right. We must each find our own way.

There may even be periods when you'll want to jump out of silence altogether and revert to your former way of praying, where you knew what you were doing and were in control. You can if you wish. But it won't be nearly as satisfying once you've tasted the sweet, mysterious silence. The author of *The Cloud of Unknowing* writes of two signs to help us recognize that God is calling us to this type of prayer:

> The interior sign is that growing desire for contemplation constantly intruding in your daily devotions.... The second sign is exterior and it manifests itself as a certain joyful enthusiasm welling up within you, whenever you hear or read about contemplation... (181).

If you are leaping out of your chair with recognition, then don't be afraid of the silence. And feel not one iota of guilt that you can't pray the way you used to, that you find yourself suddenly speechless. Your communication with God will not depend on words anymore. Like lovers who have said it all, you'll now gaze into each other's eyes.

A Special Place to Pray

"Whenever you pray, go to your room, close your door, and pray to your Father in private. Then your Father, who sees what no one sees, will repay you" (Mt 6:6).

For years I prayed in one little corner of our bedroom and dreamed of the day I would have my own prayer room. Many people don't have the luxury of a separate room they can call their own until their children are raised. Our youngest son moved out recently, and I laid claim to his room—again! There were a few short periods when I did have a prayer room, but then one or another of the kids would move back home, and I'd be praying in the corner of the bedroom again. You've heard of the "boomerangers"—adult children who move out for a time, then move back to mom and dad for financial security. All three of our kids did it, at least once. With rent high and low entry-level wages, it's difficult for young people to get started. But now they're doing fine and have been put on notice. "Next time it's the living room couch!" I have my room again—my wonderful prayer/writing/dreaming/reading/room.

You can design your own prayer room any way you want; there are no rules. Well, maybe there is just one. It has to be "you." So decorate it with your favorite colors, pictures, books, statues, flowers, anything you want. I took so much pleasure in decorating my room. As soon as I step into it I feel peaceful.

Wait. I just had a thought. I'm wondering... Do you think you would like to see my prayer room? You would? I'm deeply honored. I don't take everyone into my sacred space, you know, only "special" people, people I know will respect and appreciate it. Could I ask you one favor first though? Would you mind taking off your shoes before we enter?

Here we are. Do you like the music I've been playing? It's one of my favorite tapes. It's called *Eternal Sanctuary*. Perfect music for "my little sanctuary." The room is small and cozy, painted pure white. To the left of the door is a large bulletin board. Here's a poster I tacked on it with this valuable advice: "To grow in contemplative prayer, try to develop a mind that does not cling to anything." Fr. Keating blessed me with this little gem in his book *Open Mind, Open Heart.* I'll talk more about this later.

There are other little sayings posted on the board and on various walls in my room, sayings I'm trying to incorporate into my subconscious mind. Here's one: "Jump into your fear and it will dissipate." And another. "Accept what is." And since I have a deadline in which to finish this book, and a tendency to get scattered, I have this poster in two places. "Stick to your intentions. Stay focused."

Over here is another message I don't want to forget. A married Catholic (formerly Episcopal) priest during a seminar on prayer said, "Pray a half-hour twice a day—It's the *only* way to grow." He is the pastor of a large parish, a husband, and father of several children, one of whom has been especially difficult to raise. If this man could pray twice a day, then I have no excuse.

Against another wall I have my personal computer and laser printer. Not only do I use it to write books and articles, I also keep (somewhat sporadically) a journal on it. Normally I don't print it out, but it's a good way of recording my inner life. A large portion of my journal consists of dreams. I date each entry and sometimes go back and scan what I've written. It helps to see what trends are developing, how my attitudes and feelings have changed over the years, and if I've learned anything.

Above the computer is a shelf that holds all my writing books, among them *Bartlett's Familiar Quotations, Queries and Submissions, Writer's Market, You Can Be a Columnist.* On the other wall, below the window that looks out to the front of the house, is a large table. All my "special" books are here, the spiritual books that have changed my life. I like to keep them close to me so I can visit them often. They're like old friends, and I simply cannot put them out of sight on the bookshelf in the closet. Even the titles make me feel close to God. *Interior Castle; The Cloud of Unknowing; Prayer that Heals Our Emotions; Born Only Once; Gift From the Sea; The Prophet; Reaching Out; The Song of the Bird,* to name a few.

My favorite picture of Jesus by female artist R. Hook hangs on one wall. It shows the loving, "human" face of Jesus. Across on the other wall is a heart-stopping picture of a very old Indian woman with deep lines in her face. The color in the background and of the frame is deep pink and purple. The old woman, her gray hair tied back in two knots, is holding her infant grandson in front of her, close to her face, looking directly into his eyes. He has jet black hair and full, chubby cheeks. Their dark eyes are locked in an eternal loving gaze.

On the floor below the picture, nestled in the corner, is one of our dining room chairs, which has been designated my prayer chair. It's a simple, straight-backed, wooden chair with an upholstered beige seat. A good prayer chair should not be too comfortable, or you'll fall asleep. Neither should it be too uncomfortable, or you won't be able to relax.

Draped over the chair is my soft prayer shawl. It's a bright, multicolored striped cloth with a deep blue, almost purple, fringe all around it. I often drape my comforting shawl around my shoulders when I pray; sometimes I place it on top of my head, then wrap it around my shoulders. It symbolizes my desire to be "clothed" with Christ. I had the shawl made especially for this purpose. I don't use it for anything else but prayer, except once I let my granddaughters play and dance on it. They had slipped it out of my room and spread it on the floor, like a magic carpet, and I almost said, "Oh, no. You can't dance on my prayer shawl." But in a moment of pure grace I saw how sacred their play was, and that I would be wise to let them bless my shawl.

On the floor next to the chair is a small, pinkish pillow with a desert southwest design that I place my bare feet on when I pray. On the other side of the pillow is an altar I fashioned out of an inexpensive round table. It's covered with a lavender cloth that matches the lavender valance on the window. I keep my Bible on it, candles, incense, and a rosary. I may adorn it with flowers at times, roses from our backyard. Some days I place an icon or statue on it, or pictures of loved ones.

Today there's a piece of braided sweet grass ("Hair of Our Mother the Earth"), burnt at one end, that Robert (my spiritual friend) and I used when we prayed together the last time he visited nearly two years ago. And the prayer card of my dear brother-in-law, Don, who died more than a year ago, sat on my altar for weeks around that first anniversary. He and I spent many hours sharing our faith, and I had a hard time letting him go. An altar is a "living" symbol of our inner life that is always changing and is precious to God.

On the other side of the altar is a large floor pillow that matches the smaller one. Sometimes I sit on the light beige carpet and rest against this pillow to read, pray, or just think. Let's see. What else can I show you? Oh, here in my closet is another stack of books I haven't read yet but plan to read in the coming months: *The Universe Story; The Artist's Way; The Portable Thoreau; Care of the Soul; Soul Mates; Legacy of the Heart; Wherever You Go, There You Are.*

While we're in here, perhaps you'd like to pray for a while. It would make me so happy—I'll even let you sit in my prayer chair. Here. Let me wrap my prayer shawl loosely around your shoulders. While you're getting comfortable, I'll light a vanilla-scented candle and put some more meditation music on for you. How about *Temple in the Forest* or maybe *Fairy Ring*? This will help quiet your mind. Later, you may not want to use any music at all, because the deep silence will be so sweet.

But for now... Relax and breathe deeply. In and out, slowly, deeply. Breathe in God's love. Breathe out tension and anxiety. Relax in the old Indian woman's loving gaze. Let yourself go deeper and deeper into God's peace.

Wandering Thoughts

I've heard people say they have given up contemplative prayer because no matter what they did, they just could not clear their minds of thoughts. They wrongfully assumed that contemplatives are able to simply sit down, make their minds blank, and immediately move into some sort of ecstatic state. First of all, it's impossible to make your mind completely blank. Even when you think you've done it, you're thinking, "My mind is finally empty of thoughts." But what about your thought that your mind is

finally empty of thoughts? Eddie Ensley, who has written extensively about contemplative prayer, states:

> This haze of thoughts was with us all along, buried deep
> within us, with a good strong cork stopping up the bottle.
> They were there unnoticed causing irritability, high blood
> pressure, and fatigue. In meditation, you allow God to
> uncork you and a parade of cloudy images and thoughts
> marches by.

Have you ever been to a parade and become bored with it? I
have. And there I am. There's nothing I can do to stop the parade,
so I have to endure it. My body is there, but I'm not. My attention
is somewhere else. It's much the same with prayer. Your wandering thoughts are trying everything they can to get your attention,
but you just let them come and let them go.

At some point, an especially dazzling, noisy, glittery thought
does grab you, and you are caught up in it for a moment. When
you become aware that you have followed this thought, well, just
let it go, let it pass down the street along with the rest of the
parade. That's all you do with wandering thoughts. Just let them
go gently, one after another, and soon the parade will be over.
You'll have moved into a place of deep silence. But then again,
every parade I've been to has had a few stragglers. Just when I
thought the parade was over, I'd hear more music. And from
around the corner and down the street comes another float,
another band, a few more clowns. They were lagging behind the
rest, and now you have to wait for *them* to pass!

Be patient. Endure it all. Let it come and go until one day you'll
learn how to ignore the whole parade. And please don't think
you've been wasting time waiting for the parade to end so you
can begin to pray. You've been praying all along!

Fr. Keating, in *Open Mind, Open Heart*, likens our thoughts to a
river with many boats passing by. He writes:

> That your superficial faculties are aware of a lot of boats and

debris coming down the stream of consciousness does not mean that your other faculties, intellect, and will, are not deeply recollected in God. You may be painfully aware of unwanted thoughts going by and wish they were not there. At the same time you may be aware that something inside of you is absorbed by a mysterious presence that is completely intangible, refined, and delicate (60).

So don't let the wandering thoughts upset you. And don't think you have to make a judgment about them, such as trying to keep the good thoughts and eliminating the bad. It's best to treat them equally. Let them all come and let them all go.

A Sacred Word

An effective way of dealing with wandering thoughts is to use a sacred word or phrase (often referred to as a mantra). Ask the Holy Spirit to give you a mantra and begin to use it whenever you notice a thought or worry taking over. Words like God, Jesus, Father, Mother, Friend, Love, Peace, Calm, Spirit are examples, but you can use anything you feel inspired to use. Fr. Keating's advice is to settle on one word or phrase early on and stick with it. Then after praying for weeks or months, it will become woven into your subconscious and rise up spontaneously.

When I first asked the Holy Spirit for my sacred phrase or mantra, I started to say, "Jesus, my Lord." And as the word "Lord" was in my mouth and on my tongue, it changed as I was saying it—to "Love." God knew that love was the word I needed to fill my spirit. So for years I used, "Jesus, my Love, Jesus, my Love, Jesus, my Love."

After a long time of praying, however, I found that even my sacred phrase became a distraction. Now I don't use a mantra at all. When I notice I'm caught up in some thought, I focus my attention on my breath, especially as it moves in and out of my nostrils. This brings me back to the present moment and leads me down again into silence. You can use breathing in the same way you use a sacred word. As soon as you notice you're thinking, gently let the thought pass by. It's not necessary to "wrestle" it away, but ever so softly return your attention to your breath. In and out, through your nostrils, down deep into your body, down to your toes.

When you are just beginning to experience contemplative prayer, you may want to say your sacred word over and over for a while in your mind. Then, as you begin to experience stillness, you might drop it until you feel distracted. Again use your sacred word or phrase to help you return your attention to God. After you've done this for some months, your sacred word will become so much a part of you that it will begin to repeat by itself. It will seem to have become part of your heartbeat.

While you may become somewhat expert in using your sacred word and keeping your attention focused, becoming adept at some sort of exercise or discipline is not the goal. The goal is to use whatever discipline you can to awaken you to the reality of God present within you. For it is friendship we desire, intimacy, a love relationship with our creator. As Fr. Keating points out, "Centering prayer is not a relaxation exercise although it may bring relaxation. It is the exercise of our personal relationship with God" (46).

Whether you decide to use a sacred word, or your breath, or even an image such as a favorite statue or picture of Christ, to help you with wandering thoughts is not all that important. It is secondary to your desire to develop a deep friendship with God. All the techniques in the world won't make us friends of God. Only the Holy Spirit can do that. Our part is to be faithful to our commitment, to not turn back when we think we're going nowhere. That's really the idea of it all anyway... to go nowhere.

The Dry Spells

Falling in love with God is much like falling in love with anyone else. In the beginning it's fireworks, bells, and sweet feelings. It's walking on clouds. It's forgetting yourself and becoming totally absorbed in the "other." It's a honeymoon we think will last forever. But as we all know, honeymoons end. They have to end. We couldn't survive a honeymoon that lasts forever—at least not in this world. And while it may seem we're slipping away from God because our feelings are calming down, in reality our relationship is growing deeper. That is, of course, if we continue to pray even when we think God has abandoned us.

This is especially difficult for people like me who've had a strong conversion experience. I didn't know what was happening. I wondered where God had gone. Didn't God love me any more? Fortunately, and not a moment too soon, I read the *Dark Night of the Soul*. There seemed to be a natural progression in prayer, stages one could almost expect. St. John of the Cross writes:

> When they are going about these spiritual exercises with the greatest delight and pleasure, and when they believe that the sun of Divine favour is shining most brightly upon them, God turns all this light of theirs into darkness, and shuts against them the door and the source of the sweet spiritual water which they were tasting in God whensoever and for as long as they desired... God now sees that they have grown a little, and are becoming strong enough to lay aside their swaddling clothes and be taken from the gentle breast; so He sets them down from His arms and teaches them to walk on their own feet; which they feel to be very strange, for everything seems to be going wrong with them (pp. 62–63).

How consoling it was to learn that God was still with me, but silent now, standing in the shadows, hoping I would begin to trust in our friendship, hoping I would grow into a spiritual "adult." I needed to love God for God, just as God is. Why did I always expect gifts? And why did I need so much reassurance? God wanted to know if I would be faithful in the dark, dry times as well as in the bright, sweet times.

In some way this reminds me of my three granddaughters. Many grandparents lavish gifts on their grandchildren. With every visit they bring something, even if it's only a candy bar or pack of gum. Rick and I never did that, and I guess I must have felt a little guilty about it. One day I said to our daughter, "You know the reason dad and I don't bring the kids gifts all the time is because we want them to be happy just to be with us. We don't want them to anticipate our visits because they think they're going to get a gift."

She agreed. "Mom, they *are* happy just to be with you." Of course, there are gifts on their birthdays, Christmas, and "special" occasions, but mostly *we* want to be their gifts. We want them to remember how we spent time with them, played cards, told stories, and just loved them. I want them to remember our little ritual: we darken the bedroom, light candles, play classical music, and three little girls and "Grandma" dance. There are no rules. It's all freeflow, whatever they feel like doing. Maybe one will crawl up onto the king-size bed and suddenly she's a fairy princess, waving her magic wand, ushering commands to us, her willing subjects. We all get into the story, which can change from one moment to the next.

At some point, when they're dancing and playing, I fade into the background. I sit in the corner and just watch, totally captivated by their beauty and imagination. After a while they get so caught up in their play and fantasies they don't even know I'm in the room. But every so often, because I can't resist, I sweep one up, and then another, to give them a hug and kiss. Soon they're back to their play and I'm back in the corner, watching them with a smile on my face. They are my pure delight, and they're not even aware of my presence.

So I can understand why God withholds spiritual consolation for long periods of time. God wants a "relationship." God wants to dance with us in the dark. God wants to visit with us every day. Some days we'll play. Other days we'll tell stories. And there will be days we'll run out of words and simply sit together, content in each other's presence. At times you may feel like you're playing alone. You may feel as though you're telling your precious stories to the wall, or as if you're just wasting time. But know that God is there, delighting in you, grateful that you still come to visit, especially now when the gifts have all but disappeared.

How does one survive the dry spells? I get through them by consciously "remembering" what happened in the beginning. I recall the honeymoon. I know what happened to me was real, and I've been able to say, "Dear God, thank you for the many spiritual consolations you've given me. I'll always remember and treasure them. But if you decide not to give me another sweet feeling, it will be all right with me. Because I still have you, God, and you're all I really want."

There Is Also Good News

Now, just when I've got you thoroughly depressed, I want to give you some good news. God does come back. There are moments when God simply cannot resist sweeping you up and showing you how deeply you are loved. And you'll experience the spiritual embrace that will heal you and take you through the next dry spell. It may not come during your time of prayer but will happen when you least expect it. It may be when you're driving to work, giving your children a bath, or balancing your checkbook. You never know when God will surprise you.

The unknown author of _The Cloud of Unknowing_ has much to say about this. It's a little difficult reading for our times because of the exclusive language; however, the material is so rich I offer it here and highly recommend that you read the entire book.

Fear not.... Even though you think you have great reason to fear. Do not panic. Instead, keep in your heart a loving trust in our Lord.... Truly, he is not far away and perhaps at any moment he will turn to you touching you more intensely than ever in the past with a quickening of the contemplative grace. Then for as long as it remains, you will think you are healed and that all is well. But when you least expect, it will be gone again, and again you will feel abandoned.... Still, do not lose heart. I promise you he will return and soon. In his own time he will come. Mightily and more wonderfully than ever before he will come to your rescue and relieve your anguish. As often as he goes, he will come back. And if you will manfully suffer it all with gentle love, each coming will be more marvelous and more joyful than the last (184).

These are powerful and consoling words. Still, it doesn't change my stance. I don't expect God to sweep me off my feet anymore. But from time to time, out of the blue, something wonderful happens—like the contemplative retreat where I experienced deep inner healing. That happened after my initial conversion experience followed by a period of dryness. I didn't think anything could have touched me as much as the first encounter, but the contemplative retreat was much more powerful. Perhaps it was because I had grown a bit and had a larger capacity for the gifts of the Spirit.

St. Teresa of Avila explains this beautifully in her classic *Interior Castle*. "It is clear that a dilation or enlargement of the soul takes place, as if the water proceeding from the spring had no means of running away, but the fountain had a device ensuring that, the more freely the water flowed, the larger became the basin" (90).

The best way to approach prayer is with an attitude of openness and gratitude. We leave our expectations outside the door, right along with our shoes. And we come into our sacred space—day after day, week after week—persevering, no matter what. If God lavishes us with gifts we say, "Thank you, God. Oh, thank you, thank you, thank you." If we go through long, grueling dry spells, we say, "Thank you, God. Oh, thank you, thank you, thank you."

Why should our response be any different? The dry spells are just as much a gift as spiritual consolation, because it's all part of an exquisite pattern. God knows what we need and what is best for our spiritual development. Our part is so simple—we just need to show up and breathe. We need only be still and quiet, as we offer the fabric of our lives to God. Then God can weave us perfectly, spacing just the right touches of dark thread against the light that will accent and add richness to the overall design.

Take comfort in the knowledge that you are growing and expanding, even when you feel absolutely nothing. And that God is smiling lovingly upon you, even more anxious than you for the next embrace.

Reading Scripture

When I attended the first retreat and later the contemplative retreat, I noticed how many people had Bibles with them, and how the retreat leaders spoke so much about Scripture. Many participants carried well-worn Bibles with tattered, marked-up pages. Mine was brand new and had never been used. It would not have occurred to me to bring a Bible if someone hadn't suggested it. They said the New American translation was preferred for the first retreat. I had tried from time to time over the years to read the Bible, but it just didn't make any sense to me. Of course, I only had an old "family Bible" that had a fancy gold cover. And it had the old language with words like "sayeth" and "goeth" and all sorts of other "eths."

But after my conversion, it became obvious that the way I would develop this new-found friendship with God would be through reading Scripture. I was intimidated by it and didn't know where to begin. I skirted around it for months and months. I read all sorts of little booklets about how to read the Bible. I learned that the Bible was a collection of books; I had always thought it was just one. I learned that there was an oral tradition first, and the gospels were written long after Jesus had died. I learned that many of the writings were slanted towards certain Christian communities, addressing the difficulties they were experiencing at the time. I also learned that after you read the Bible for a while, the Holy Spirit would be present in a special way to teach you personally.

For a long time, perhaps six or more months, I read all these booklets about reading Bible without ever turning one page in the Bible! I think I was afraid it would leave me cold again as it had in the past, and that the booklets would not live up to their promises. Finally, I picked up my New American Bible that was written in modern language. It was time to dive in. Enough with all the little instructional booklets. I was still apprehensive. Would it really be all they said it would be? Would it be relevant to me? Now? Yes, yes, and yes.

There's power in the Word, more power than I ever would have imagined. I came to know Jesus, and Jesus showed me a God I never knew, a God who loved me. Little by little, I read. Some passages were too deep for me, and I didn't grasp them in the beginning. Others came at me with so much energy I felt they were written just for me.

I read the Bible for years before I realized I wasn't simply reading. I was being fed and nourished, loved and taught. I was being given strength and insight, and even a bit of wisdom. It happened a little at a time, in small, bite-size meals. It was food for my soul, and I had been digesting it slowly.

Some days I wouldn't pick up my Bible. There were periods when I didn't pick it up for weeks if my life grew too busy. But the Word had been sown in my heart and was growing without my awareness. When I needed it, it would surface—the right verse, the right parable, the right psalm. It was all there.

I remember as if it were yesterday when a friend of mine phoned to tell me about the fabulous new house she and her husband had just bought. I congratulated her and chatted for a while. Then when I hung up I was suddenly green with envy. I wanted a new house too. I fussed about it for a while, not liking myself very much for feeling the way I did. Then I heard in my mind, and quite firmly too, "Store up heavenly treasure" (Mt 6:20). Experiences like this have happened to me over and over. The Word is alive with the power to change us! But we have to know it first, digest it, and let it do its work.

If you haven't taken up the Bible in a long time, or if it has disappointed you in the past, try it again. Get a translation with modern language. Then jump in. Don't get stuck like I did in the instruction manuals. Yes, it's good to know how to read the Bible. It's even good to take an in-depth Bible studies class, which I eventually did. But don't deprive yourself of the magnificent riches of Scripture for one moment longer than you have to. Don't wait. Your soul needs food.

Friends for the Journey

Friends. What would we do without them? There's a wonderful song we sing in church that always seems to touch me. It's about sharing our walk. And the one line that always gets to me is, "You give wonderful comrades to me." I wrote in my second book, *Womanprayer/Spiritjourney,*

> Thank you, God, for providing me with wonderful comrades who share my journey. Friends who understand the exhilaration, the pitfalls, the mundaneness, the surprises, the aridity, the joy, and the pain of following you. For wouldn't I die in the desert if there was no one who understood? (33)

We need friends for this journey, for it is like no other. We need soul friends, companions who are on the same road. So we must pray for guidance and look for a small praying community to join. One reason is that when we move into deeper prayer we may have an ecstatic experience and be tempted to think we're "special" and better than others. But when we meet with people who are also on a profound journey, we discover the outrageous generosity of God. Then our experience can be seen in perspective.

Also, as you go deeper and begin to experience inner healing, you may have a disturbing experience, or your first dry spell, or perhaps you just can't seem to stay committed. This is where your small group can help. Someone has been right where you are. You'll find answers in your group, as well as insight and wisdom. Because that's how God works. "Where two or three are gathered in my name, there am I in their midst" (Mt 18:20).

Many parishes are very large. It's difficult to get the nourishment we need from attending Sunday services alone. I want to point out, however, that the practice of private daily prayer greatly enhances the experience of communal prayer. The first Mass I attended after my conversion was rich and full of meaning for me. My eyes were riveted to the crucifix hovering over the altar. The liturgical prayers were penetrating, as though I'd never heard them before. There was spiritual power in the music, and I found myself singing as if I were caught up in a universal choir encompassing past and present, heaven and earth, saints, angels, and "holy men and women" of every age. Of course, this was in my "honeymoon" stage, and I had a heightened sense of awareness. Naturally my feelings have calmed down, but the Mass and Eucharist have remained central to my faith. My daily prayer builds through the week, culminating in the great prayer of the eucharist on Sunday mornings.

Having said all this, I still believe it is important to augment our Sunday worship with another weekly or monthly gathering with a small group. There is a national network of centering prayer groups you may be interested in. These groups meet once a month to pray and learn, and are committed to ongoing spiritual formation. You'll find people from all walks of life there—some beginners in prayer, others more advanced and able to mentor novices. (To find a centering prayer group near your home, call or write: Contemplative Outreach, Ltd., National Office, 9 William St./P.O. Box 737, Butler, New Jersey 07405 (201) 838-3384.)

Finding spiritual companions for the journey is essential, because when you move into deeper prayer it's not good to be off on your own. Without mature guides, you can easily become unbalanced. And we've all heard of entire groups becoming unbalanced by following the wrong guides. It's best to be connected to one of the mainstream churches that has deep roots. If you're Catholic, perhaps you've never delved too deeply into your heritage. I was surprised and delighted to learn my spiritual genealogy. My heritage as a Catholic is rich and diverse. And while there is much in the institutional, hierarchical church that upsets me, still, it is my home. I feel intimately connected to the early Christians and the great saints who have gone before me, and the symbols and rituals of the church are so much a part of my religious identity that I would be lost without them.

So it's good if your "small church" is affiliated with a larger church. That doesn't mean all members have to be Catholic, or Methodist, or Lutheran. But just as it's not good for one person to take the spiritual journey alone, the same holds true for a small faith community. A small group operates best and all its members develop in a healthy, sound manner when the group is drawing from some great spiritual well, from some great body of faith that has been handed down for generations and has stood the test of time.

So now, here you are. You've prayed and felt drawn to a certain small faith community. At first it may all seem rosy. You're delighted you've found the perfect group, but there is no perfect group. You knew that. You just thought this one would be different. But even this group is made up of imperfect people on the road to perfection. So in no time at all you begin to see the warts. And you may decide you don't want to work so hard at this; you may think it's easier to go it alone. And it may be. But you won't make as much progress, because we grow from bumping up against each other, scrapping a little now and then. And we learn things in a group we could never learn on our own.

God calls us as a people, not a person. So stick with it, persevere in the good times and the bad, just as you do in prayer. And watch, just watch and be amazed, how the group and all its members mature. And be astonished at how those whom you thought you could never understand, let alone love, become dear to you. God is in your midst, and whispering secrets in your ear. A new compassion and understanding will take root in your heart. "And she [Wisdom], who is one, can do all things, and renews everything while herself perduring; And passing into holy souls from age to age, she produces friends of God and prophets" (Wis 7:27).

She produced you—a friend of God.

Meditation

Sit quietly now, with your eyes closed. Relax and begin to breathe deeply...in and out...slowly, deeply. Settle into God's peace and loving presence. Breathe out anxiety and fear. Breathe in calm and silence. Let the silence be thick and soft. Picture it as a warm, yellow blanket that will comfort you and keep you safe. Ask God to give you a word—"your" word. Repeat it now, slowly, gently, effortlessly. Let every thought come and go, even the sweet thoughts. Don't wrestle with them. When you notice a thought, simply let it pass before you and return to your sacred word. And if your word seems to get lost, then let it go, too, along with every thought. Rest in God's love and peace for as long as you wish.

CHAPTER SEVEN

SPIRITUAL FRIENDS

Earlier I described my powerful experience at the contemplative retreat conducted by Eddie Ensley and Robert Herrmann. Several months after the retreat, when my tears dried up and I had a better understanding of the inner healing that had taken place, I wrote to them. I had a strong feeling that I needed to express how important their work was. And as it turned out they needed the affirmation, because their ministry was unusual. They had taken an incredible step of faith.

Eddie Ensley is a man of courage and vision. He founded a Catholic community of laymen known as Contemplative Brothers, who are dedicated to a celibate life-style of prayer, study, and action. In some ways this group resembles a religious order, but it is not one. While not common today, in the early church there were many such communities of celibates who became strong spiritual friends. Eddie and Robert have based much of their ministry on this tradition, having read the writings of St. Paulinas of Nola, St. Bernard of Clairvaux, and others.

Their ministry started out with a great emphasis on contemplation and our rich Christian heritage, going back to the Middle Ages and to the Church Fathers. They discovered that as they talked out of this rich material, people were being healed. Part of my healing on my retreat weekend with them had to do with the connections I felt with all those who had gone before me.

The "Brothers" responded to my letter with gratitude and said they had heard from others who made that retreat who also had strong experiences. They said that for them, too, it had been perhaps the most powerful retreat they had ever given.

Robert told me that he is an introvert and shy, and that it was so out of character for him to come down from that podium to embrace me. Especially extending his arms the way he did, but he was strongly moved to do it. After that, Robert and I started exchanging letters, then phone calls. In time, a wonderful spiritual friendship developed. Robert (who is nearly 40 now) and I have been friends for twenty years! It's been wonderful, rocky, joyful, exasperating, challenging, heavenly, all-out war, uplifting, maddening, and one of the greatest gifts of my life. Robert and I know, beyond the shadow of a doubt, we are called to be spiritual friends.

What an odd couple we make. Robert is a celibate layman living in a Catholic community, and I am a married woman, mother, now grandmother, eighteen years his senior. Robert's an introvert; I'm an extrovert. He lives in Georgia, and I live in Arizona. Yet we have maintained a long-distance friendship all these years.

There seem to be no rules in spiritual friendship. By that I mean the friends could be two females, two males, a male and female, married or single, young or old. Gender, race, age, station in life do not seem to matter, because our essence is spirit—ageless, colorless, genderless. So if you are called to a spiritual friendship, don't shy away from it just because you don't look like a match. But you need to be cautious, of course, and seek good counsel, especially if one or both parties are married. And everyone should know one another, including children if there are any. All should be brought into the circle of friendship. Trust is built through spending time together, sharing meals, prayer and laughter.

In the early years my husband had to do a real stretch, but God bless him, he did it. I'll never forget what he said to me one day. "Judy, I don't understand this, but I trust you and I trust them." (He was including Eddie, who has been my mentor and dear friend.) This made me love my husband all the more, because what he was saying was, "I respect you and will support you in your spiritual journey, even though I don't know where it will take you."

If Rick and I didn't have a strong marriage, this friendship would not have been possible. Spiritual friendship with the opposite sex is not a good idea if one or both of the parties are in shaky marriages or relationships. A good test of whether the friendship is from God is if both parties are becoming more committed to their primary relationship, that is, their spouse or religious community, etc.

My relationship with Robert only made my relationship with my husband and children better, stronger, and much more loving. This became evident to all of us. The respect and trust we've all been able to show for one another (Rick, Eddie, Robert, myself, and even our children) has truly been an inspiration to me. God has been in our midst, stretching us all.

Learning About This Friendship

When we first became friends, Robert and I were both a little nervous. I didn't know anything about spiritual friendship. I had to learn about it, because it's not an ordinary friendship. What do spiritual friends do? It didn't take long to figure out. We simply talked—about everything—our dreams, our childhood, our feelings, plans, hopes, and goals. Spiritual friends share insights, observe patterns they see emerging in one another. They read Scripture to each other, talk about the spiritual books they're reading, share parts of their journal, talk about the pain in the world, intercede together for that pain.

They take each other to task when necessary. Robert and I keep each other praying. We feel a responsibility to help each other mature, both spiritually and emotionally. I've affirmed Robert in his ministry on days when he thought he was throwing his life away. I've reminded him of all the people he has helped, all the people he and Eddie have taught how to pray. He has affirmed me and shown me how my gifts were maturing when I could see no growth. He's gifted me with the fruits of his enormously deep prayer life, with a wisdom that's always been far beyond his chronological age.

When I first met Robert I hardly ever read the newspaper, let alone a serious book. I was a busy working mother barely keeping my head above water. I didn't want to know about the suffering of the world. It was suffering enough to get out of bed on Monday morning and face another busy week. But maybe I was where I was supposed to be, because I believe there are times when all that God expects of us is to attend to the immediate needs of our family.

However, the children were growing older, and I still didn't have much of a social conscience. Robert tugged, cajoled, nudged, and sometimes pushed me into the pain of the world. It was hard for me, because my prayer had deepened and my heart was more tender. I couldn't look at the images of war and starving children and battered women. It hurt too much. And I had to educate myself. That was hard, too, but Robert wouldn't give up. With great patience he waited as I grew and learned so we could discuss some of the burning issues he felt so strongly about.

That is what spiritual friends do. They fill in each other's gaps so both can move on to wholeness. For that's when God can use them most effectively.

The following is a beautiful passage about spiritual friendship written around 1150 A.D. by Aelred of Rieraulx. Eddie Ensley has a tremendous gift of digging up these treasures. Through his scholarly study he has unearthed for many the rich tradition of the Catholic Church. Here is one of many gems he's given me that has made me appreciate the wealth of my spiritual heritage. It's called "The Beauty of Friendship."

The sweetness of God that we taste in this life is given us, not so much for enjoyment as for a consolation and encouragement for our weakness. That is why it is such a great joy to have the consolation of someone's affection—someone to whom one is deeply united by the bonds of love; someone in whom our weary spirit may find rest, and to whom we may pour out our souls... someone whose conversation is as sweet as a song in the tedium of our daily life. He must be someone whose soul will be to us a refuge to creep into when the world is altogether too much for us; someone to whom we can confide all our thoughts. His spirit will give us the comforting kiss that heals all the sickness of our preoccupied hearts.

He will weep with us when we are troubled, and rejoice with us when we are happy, and he will always be there to consult when we are in doubt. And we will be so deeply bound to him in our hearts that even when he is far away, we shall find him together with us in spirit, together and alone. The world will fall asleep all round you, you will find, and your soul will rest, embraced in absolute peace. Your two hearts will lie quiet together, united as if they were one, as the grace of the Holy Spirit flows over you both.

This beautiful passage would make anyone want to run after spiritual friendship. And you may be wondering if it is for everyone. I honestly don't know. I don't believe it's something you can seek out on your own like ordinary friendships. You can pray for it, and be open to it, but you can't make it happen. Those who are meant to be spiritual friends just seem to find each other at the right time. And when it happens, it may be so strange that you know it couldn't possibly have been your idea. But even if you're convinced it's from God, don't go too fast. You're moving into holy space. Eddie puts it so beautifully: "Like all of God's treasures, spiritual friendship should be approached slowly, like inching on one's knees in a cathedral."

Ultimately, spiritual friendship is a calling. And it's a commitment, because God has plans for spiritual friends. Much good has come from my relationship with Robert. This is my fourth book, and I wonder if I would have become a writer had I not met him. I don't think so, but if I did I'm certain my writing would have been shallow and perhaps not even publishable.

Robert says his ministry has also had more depth and richness because I've helped him understand and develop his feminine side. And I continue to "nag" him to write spiritual books, because I recognized his writing talent years ago. I've also helped keep him in touch with "real life" and in tune with the "ordinary" people he ministers to, because I've been a busy working woman with a husband and three children. Our house, which he and Eddie have visited many times, is quite different from theirs. They live a quiet life of prayer, solitude, and study, blessing thousands (including myself) with the fruits this kind of life produces. So our life-styles complement each other. We move each other to the center where we're more apt to be balanced and emotionally healthy.

There are many wonderful benefits that come from a committed, long-term spiritual friendship. If you think you're called, it would be a good idea to consult with a spiritual director, because it's a delicate relationship, especially in the early years. But God expects us to receive the gift with gratitude and treat it responsibly, with utmost respect, because it's more than a friendship. It's not just for you and your friend to enjoy the sweet conversation and to pour out your souls to each other, lovely as that is.

God wants to use you, but first you must grow. God wants you to blossom and achieve your full potential, and a good spiritual friend will want that for you too.

Spiritual Directors

Spiritual directors are not the same as spiritual friends. A spiritual director usually has many people to direct and couldn't possibly become intimate friends with all of them. And if the director did become your close friend it would impede your progress, because sometimes a spiritual director may have to say hard things, like, "The honeymoon ends. It's supposed to end. Do you love God only because of the good feelings? Because of the gifts? Do you love God because of the spiritual highs that make you feel giddy and in love with the whole world? Will you love God now that you have some hard work to do?"

The hard work, the spiritual development, has a lot to do with working on our relationships. A spiritual director can be invaluable in helping us understand this connection. The challenge, however, is to find someone you'll click with. We all have different personalities, and just because two people are dedicated to God doesn't necessarily mean they're going to get along.

Say you do find a director. Maybe someone has given this person á glowing recommendation and you start going to see him or her. If after a few sessions you discover you're a bit uncomfortable, don't be afraid to say you think you should find someone else. Spiritual directors are professionals and want the very best for you. Chances are he or she already knew the two of you were not a good match. There are reasons we don't yet understand why a person can be so much in sync with one person and so completely out of sync with another. I think much of it has to do with unseen vibrations, our energy field. I know this sounds New Age, but there is much about our being we simply do not understand.

I used to work with a woman who completely baffled me. She was bright, friendly, and interesting, but I could never get on the same wavelength as she. When I started to speak, she'd step on my words. When she started, I'd step on hers, because I never knew when she was finished. I felt like I was playing jump rope, double dutch, swaying my body back and forth trying to find the right moment to hop in. There was really nothing wrong with either one of us except our "vibrations" or wavelengths weren't synchronized. So don't stay with a director if you're uncomfortable. You need to feel as though you're connecting on a deep level.

Another thing to consider when choosing a spiritual director is gender. Over the years I've had male directors and female, and for me, female is definitely the best. You'll have to decide for yourself. I used to think I had to have a priest director. I tried two of them, and you know what? They didn't understand me!

You may have a different experience, but I've found there are things women can say to other women that will be immediately understood. You can tell by the way they nod their heads or the look in their eyes. You can just feel it—they've been there. Yes, a man might possibly understand, but it will be a stretch. And you don't have time for stretches. You want to grow! Also, there's the sexual energy between a male and female. You know it's there. And it sometimes gets in the way.

It's my opinion that men, too, would be better off with male directors. Even though some men prefer women for spiritual directors because they see it as an opportunity to develop their feminine side, there may be times a female director will have to stretch to understand them. After all, women grew up as little girls, not little boys. (I hope my feminist friends won't come after me for this.) But from my own experience and from talking to other women, I think it's true.

When our son was growing up, I always felt a little tentative about what he was experiencing. I wasn't sure how he felt. Not so for our two daughters; I knew what they were experiencing. I had once been a little girl.

Whether you choose a male or female is up to you. The most important thing, however, is to find someone you can be perfectly honest with, because the process will only work if you can let all facets of your personality emerge. In the beginning, I only showed my spiritual director my sweet, religious face. "Here I am. Look at me. I pray, I work at church, I volunteer for everything, I'm Super Mom." I only began to make progress when I allowed my other faces and other voices to surface, the ones I don't really like very much, the ones I may even loathe.

As you can see, the job of a spiritual director is extremely challenging. That's why the people who do this work need to be highly trained for it. They've spent a lot of years in study; therefore, they need to charge for their time. I think most people are surprised by this. But think of it. Would you like to spend hours every week doing difficult work like this with no compensation? Many spiritual directors are nuns or laymen and women who work in the church. They are woefully underpaid, and many supplement their income by doing spiritual direction. Their fees may vary. Many take directees on a sliding scale according to what they can afford. Personally, I think it's worth sacrificing a lot to be able to afford a spiritual director.

They help you make sense of your life. They mirror back to you what you already know but don't quite know how to say. A good spiritual director helps you recognize your potential and helps you to blossom much faster than you would on your own.

Meditation

Take some time to reflect on your friendships. Are there people in your life with whom you can share your spiritual dreams? Do you have a mentor to walk with you on this incredible journey?

If not, you may want to call your parish or a retreat center and ask for help in finding a spiritual director. And if you're searching for "soul friends," take a few moments and reflect on what it would be like to have a friend "whose soul will be to us a refuge to creep into when the world is altogether too much for us; someone to whom we can confide all our thoughts...."

Sit quietly and imagine you are in sweet spiritual conversation with such a friend. But don't picture that friend in terms of physical body. Instead sense the love and caring your friend has for you. You feel so comfortable, completely relaxed with your friend. There is no fear about how you look or what you might say.

You can cry or laugh, whatever you need to do. You can be playful, even silly with your friend. Being with your friend is almost like being with Jesus. You feel totally loved and accepted, just as you are at this very moment.

Ask God to send the right friend to you, someone who will see your goodness and help you develop your gifts and talents, someone who will stick with you, through thick and thin, on your long spiritual journey.

So now...the seed has been planted, the request made. Be patient in the coming months. Don't try to force this kind of friendship. Simply be open to it, and if it is meant to happen, it will.

CHAPTER EIGHT

LIVING IN
THE PRESENT MOMENT

There are times in our lives when we are too busy to pray, and there's nothing we can do about it. We may be working a lot of overtime or caring for a seriously ill family member. During these periods, we won't have to feel like our prayer life is lagging if we practice living in the present moment.

In an earlier chapter, when I described my prayer room, I pointed out the poster that says: "To grow in contemplative prayer, try to develop a mind that does not cling to anything." This quote, borrowed from the *Diamond Sutra*, was taken from Fr. Keating's book *Open Mind, Open Heart*. When I first read it, I felt a great relief. Ostensibly, it was giving me permission to let go of all my rambling thoughts, thoughts I used to think I had to deal with and make sense of.

In those few simple words, I was given a wonderful gift. I now had a sure formula, not only for spiritual growth but for emotional health as well (one could reasonably argue these are one and the same). I made the sign because I never wanted to forget this valuable advice. Then I began to practice it every day. I'm sure it was meant not only for the time we actually pray but for the whole of our lives. It can become a permanent practice that will eventually free us. Ironically, it will free us from ourselves!

I've added another saying to it. I use it a lot when I feel myself going into my "poor me" routine, the whiny one that says, "It's not fair." "I don't deserve this." "After all I've done for you." Do you know that one? Now when I see it coming, I try to ward it off with my secret weapon, "Let it come and let it go." I've said these words so many times in the past few years they have become part of my unconscious. Often when I'm disturbed, the words rise up on their own, "Let it come and let it go. Let it come and let it go. Let it come and let it go."

So much of what plagues us are thoughts of past hurts, an accumulation of little things that were said or done over a lifetime. Even if we were to confront those who have offended us, they may have no recollection of the incident and may even deny it ever happened. Then where would we be? People remember things differently. Just sit among seven or eight siblings who grew up in the same home and ask them about their childhood. You'll swear they couldn't possibly have come from the same environment. They must have had different parents!

Perhaps you still think you would feel better if you could just tell someone from the past just how much they hurt you. In some instances that may be appropriate. But I'm not talking about grievous wrongs like child abuse. Of course, that would need attention and the help of a spiritual director or professional counselor. Usually, however, the clutter in our minds consists mostly of hurtful things that were said or thoughtless actions that affected us. And if we insist on bringing them out in the open, and the person is someone close to us, like a parent or sibling, it may cause more harm than good. Another thing to remember is that we, too, have offended others. Maybe not deliberately, but nevertheless, we've hurt people. Would we want to be confronted years later? Or do we pray in our hearts that the whole thing has been forgotten? Do we pray secretly for compassion and forgiveness? I know I do.

So what do we do with those thoughts that spring up unexpectedly, unannounced, and uninvited? I've found the best way to loosen their grip is not to cling to them, but to simply say, "Let it come and let it go." Notice I don't say, "Don't let it come," but, "Let it come." I don't want to get into the business of repression, which is unhealthy. So I let everything come and let most everything go. If something persists, then I know it needs my attention. I think we can all recognize the important things that require work, but 99% of what clutters our minds is not worth two seconds of our attention. And the sooner we let such thoughts move off the projection screen of our minds, the better off we'll be.

At first it may seem strange. We're so used to grabbing onto our thoughts, entering into old conversations, changing the outcome to suit us. But it's all fantasy. It's not real! What happened, happened. Why waste precious energy trying to change what cannot be changed? In the beginning it will take a conscious effort to let go, but after a while you'll do it automatically. This is one of the best habits one could ever develop, because it brings emotional healing and great peace. But it will take a little time and a lot of practice, to keep coming back to now. If you think of God as being here in the present moment, and nowhere else, you'll want to be here, too.

Practice... Practice... Practice

Letting go of the blizzard of thoughts that clutters one's inner world takes practice. So be patient with yourself, because you're in the messy process of reprogramming your mind. I'm fascinated with computers and often use them as analogies. I've worked in several law firms during times when they completely changed their computer systems. This process was always one big headache for everyone. Even though the old operating systems were out-of-date and inefficient compared to the new, most of the staff didn't want to change. They were comfortable with the old way; they knew how things worked.

But along come the computer technicians. They unhook the old computer and cart it away, and a little bit of you goes with it. You know that soon you're going to look and feel stupid! Soon you'll be frustrated and find yourself talking back to this new-fangled computer with its jillion windows as it "prompts" you with online messages. And you'll fight it. Darn it! You don't need any computer that thinks it's smarter than you to tell you how to operate.

But then one day you realize, begrudgingly, that if you'll only follow the instructions you'll get wonderful, amazing results. Little by little you regain your confidence. Yes. I can do this! And in just a few weeks you notice your work is cut nearly in half. You're operating with ease, speed, and tremendous efficiency. While you might not admit it out loud (especially to the office manager), you know you wouldn't go back to the old system for all the money in the world.

So even though it seems odd and awkward at first, we can practice letting go, coming back to the present moment, over and over. By not clinging to anything, we learn to really live each busy moment of our lives. God is fully present in each moment, and would probably like it if we were too. You may have heard the saying, "God did not say I WAS, or I WILL BE. God said, I AM." God is I AM. God is NOW. When we practice living in the present moment, where God is, we are praying—always.

So whenever I find my thoughts scattered all over the place, I gently return to the present moment where God is, and I talk to God about everything. I try to be in constant communication with God—when I'm driving, working, whatever—I talk to God. It's not constant chatter, but more like a glance, a comment here and there, a returning to the Presence that is always with me.

It doesn't take the place of my quiet, focused prayer time, but it keeps me calm and recollected. When we learn how to "return" to God in the midst of our hectic lives, we'll understand how Paul could say, "Rejoice always, never cease praying, render constant thanks; such is God's will for you in Christ Jesus" (1 Thes 5:16–18).

Twenty Minutes Twice a Day

Praying twenty minutes in the morning and twenty minutes in the evening can change our lives forever. Yes, there are days and weeks when we simply get out of practice or really don't have time to pray. Then we have to rely on "keeping in touch" with God as stated above—returning to the present moment, talking to God constantly, finding a quiet place at lunchtime, praying in the car, in the elevator, even in the restroom at work! But the ideal way that I am always "returning to" is twice a day for a minimum of twenty minutes.

Taking twenty minutes to a half-hour morning and evening will accelerate our intimacy with God. This in turn accelerates our healing, growth, and transformation. God puts no pressure on us. It's always an invitation that we can accept or refuse. Either way, God still loves us. But the sooner we become full and healthy human beings, the sooner God can use us to help heal the world. Don't think this is for your own good alone (I believe I did at first). The more you develop, the more you realize the truth of the Scripture, "Much will be required of the person entrusted with much, and still more will be demanded of the person entrusted with more" (Lk 12:48).

What is expected is that we begin to develop our gifts and talents and put them to use in God's service. At times God will ask us to serve right in our homes: building, repairing, creating healthy relationships, and raising confident, "well-loved" children. Later we may find ourselves branching out into our larger communities. We'll learn how to discern and follow our Inner Guide who will whisper to us where we should go and what we should say. Through it all, we are moving, ever so slowly, to a higher level of consciousness.

The key to this transformation of the heart is perseverance, not giving up. Not saying, I can't get back into prayer, too much time has passed. It's just as if you've been on a diet and lost a lot of weight. But then you weaken and eat everything in sight. Well, the best thing you can do is not beat yourself up about it, but the next day get right back on the diet.

So, too, with prayer. It's important to get back to it as soon as you can. Even if you're away from regular prayer times for long stretches because of illness or severe problems, never give up! Keep going back to it, and going back, and going back. Think how God must love us when we do that. Think of how many acts of faith we make when we resist the temptation to give up prayer altogether.

Praying when it's hard to pray must make God smile tenderly upon us, especially because we're not in a cloister. And yet we make this tremendous commitment. Fr. Keating once said that laypeople can make as much spiritual progress as religious who are cloistered. Let me use his words:

> Those who do the centering prayer, faithfully, twice a day, which is a capsule of the contemplative lifestyle that is spread over the whole of life, will make the same progress as if they entered a contemplative lifestyle or cloister, and perhaps more. The reason I say this is that it is not the lifestyle that is transforming, but rather the fidelity to dismantling the false self system, and this is the result of a practice of contemplative prayer. So that one can be in a cloister without actually practicing enough discipline to initiate or to further this purification process.

If we are faithful to our quiet time, and keep coming back, after a while we become addicted to prayer and addicted to God. We simply don't feel good when we don't pray. We have withdrawal symptoms. This kind of addiction is good, because it helps to keep us coming back to our prayer space. So breathe life into that space by praying there frequently. Let it call you. And after a while, believe me, it will.

Letting Go Exercise

On a sheet of plain, white paper, write or type in large, bold letters the words:

"To grow in contemplative prayer, try to develop a mind that does not cling to anything."

On another sheet, write the words:

"Let it come and let it go."

Post these signs where you will see them every day—perhaps on your bathroom mirror. Then begin to practice letting go of all unnecessary thoughts that only clutter your mind and drain your energy. Don't let yourself get "stuck" on anything. Keep coming back to the present moment—right here, right now, where God is. At first it may seem awkward, but keep practicing. Try not to cling to anything. And after a while you'll realize how healing and energizing it is to simply let go and give it all to God.

CONCLUSION

In his book *Open Mind, Open Heart*, Fr. Keating talks about the Ten Ox Pictures of Zen. He says,

> The last one represents the return to ordinary life after full enlightenment. It symbolizes the fact that there is no way to distinguish the life with which you started from what it has become, except that it is totally transformed in its ordinariness (104).

This reminds me of the beautiful old woman I used to visit who died right before she was to turn 102. I met her on the occasion of her 100th birthday. Her caretakers at the home where she resided (having outlived her family) threw her a wonderful birthday party on the back lawn. There were balloons, delicious food, and a live band. Sara and the other elderly residents, donning party hats and dressed in their Sunday best, were thoroughly enjoying the warm air and the fine celebration when I arrived.

The band was made up of retirees. During a break, one of the musicians came up to Sara, wished her a happy birthday, then asked her how old she thought he was. She studied him for a moment, then said, "Eighty-nine?"

He was momentarily stunned, but quickly recovered and said, "Seventy-four!" To Sara, eighty-nine was young, and she probably thought she was complimenting him. He smiled at her, and moved back to the band that was starting to play "Happy Birthday to You." By the look on his face, I'm sure he was thinking he'd never again ask an old woman to guess his age!

Throughout the week, the festivities continued. Sara, an avid sports fan, received an autographed picture from her hero, football great Joe Montana; was taken by limousine to a Phoenix Suns basketball game where her name was flashed on the scoreboard several times, "Happy Birthday, Sara, 100 years old"; and was even given a write-up in the local newspaper complete with her picture. With all this attention and love, Sara glowed for months.

Then one day I visited her and she seemed a little down. "What's wrong, Sara?" I asked.

She sighed deeply, then said, "I thought something would change when I turned 100."

"Like what, Sara?"

"I don't know. I thought maybe I'd get transferred or something. Maybe I'd go to another room or eat different food. But nothing has changed."

Like Sara, perhaps we think we'll "get transferred or something" now that we've been "enlightened." But as Anthony de Mello reveals in his marvelous book *The Song of the Bird*, if we chop wood, we'll still chop wood.

When the Zen master attained enlightenment he wrote the following lines to celebrate it: "Oh wondrous marvel: I chop wood! I draw water from the well!"

After enlightenment nothing really changes. The tree is still a tree; people are just what they were before and so are you. You may continue to be as moody or even-tempered, as wise or foolish. The one difference is that you see things with a different eye. You are more detached from it all now. And your heart is full of wonder. This is the essence of contemplation: the sense of wonder (16).

So you will still continue to live your ordinary life after conversion and even after years of prayer. But it won't be the same. You will wonder and be in awe of your very own life. As time goes on, you will discover your mission, your purpose for being alive. You will marvel at the gifts God has given you, and feel deeply honored and grateful to be part of God's plan to love and heal the world.

You—a fully human "ordinary" person—have become one of the new saints, mystics, and poets of this generation... because you pray.

RESOURCES

Note: The resources below are in the order in which they appear in this book.

Esway, Judy. *Womanprayer, Spiritjourney.* Mystic, CT: Twenty-Third Publications, 1987.

The Cloud of Unknowing. Ed. William Johnston. Garden City, NY: Image Books, 1961.

Avila, St. Teresa of, *Interior Castle.* Trans. & Ed. E. Allison Peers. Garden City, NY: Image Books, 1961.

John of the Cross, *Dark Night of the Soul.* Trans. & Ed. E. Allison Peers. Garden City, NY: Image Books, 1961.

Sanford, John A. *Healing and Wholeness.* New York: Paulist Press, 1977.

Ensley, Eddie. *Prayer That Heals Our Emotions.* San Francisco: Harper & Row, 1988.

Keating, Thomas. *Open Mind, Open Heart.* Rockport, MA: Element, 1992.

Peck, M. Scott. *The Road Less Traveled.* New York: Simon & Schuster, 1978.

Esway, Judy. *Letting Go.* Mystic, CT: Twenty-Third Publications, 1990.

Bolshakoff, Sergius & Pennington, M. Basil. *In Search of True Wisdom.* New York: Doubleday, 1979.

Enzler, Clarence. *My Other Self.* Denville, NJ: Dimension Books, 1958.

Nikodimos of the Holy Mountain & Makarios of Corinth. *The Philokalia.* Trans. & Ed. G.E.H. Palmer, Philip Sherrard, & Kallistos Ware. London: Faber and Faber, 1979.

Harris, Maria. *Dance of the Spirit.* New York: Bantam, 1989.

Baars, Conrad. *Born Only Once.* Chicago, IL: Franciscan Herald Press, 1975.

de Mello, Anthony. *The Song of the Bird*. New York: Image Books, 1984.

Gibran, Kahlil. *The Prophet*. New York: Knopf, 1923, (Renewal) 1951.

Kabat-Zinn, Jon. *Wherever You Go, There You Are*. New York: Hyperion, 1994.

Lindbergh, Anne Morrow. *Gift from the Sea*. New York: Vintage, 1978.

Moore, Thomas. *Soul Mates*. New York: HarperCollins, 1994.

Moore, Thomas. *Care of the Soul*. New York: HarperCollins, 1992.

Muller, Wayne. *Legacy of the Heart*. New York: Fireside, 1992.

Nouwen, Henri J.M. *Reaching Out*. New York: Doubleday, 1975.

Rowland, Mike. "Fairy Ring." Milwaukee, WI: Distributed by Music Design, 1982.

Swimme, Brian & Berry, Thomas. *The Universe Story*. San Francisco: Harper, 1992.

Thoreau, Henry. *The Portable Thoreau*. Ed. Carl Bode. Penguin, 1983.

Of Related Interest...